C. G. JUNG:

His Friendships with Mary Mellon
and J. B. Priestley

C. G. JUNG:
His Friendships with Mary Mellon and J. B. Priestley

William Schoenl

CHIRON PUBLICATIONS • WILMETTE, ILLINOIS

Library of Congress Catalog Card Number: 98-3150

Printed in the United States of America
Designed and typeset by Sans Serif, Inc., Saline, MI

Library of Congress Cataloging-in-Publication Data

Schoenl, William J., 1941–
 C.G. Jung's friendships with Mary Mellon and J.B. Priestley / William Schoenl.
  p. cm.
  Includes bibliographical references (p.   ) and index.
  ISBN 1-888602-08-2 (alk. paper)
  1. Jung, C. G. (Carl Gustav), 1875–1961—Friends and associates. 2. Mellon, Mary, 1905–1946—Friends and associates. 3. Priestley, J. B. (John Boynton), 1894—Friends and associates. 4. Psychoanalysts—Switzerland—Biography. 5. Psychoanalysis—History. I. Title.
BF109.J8S43 1998
150.19'54'092—dc21
[B]   98-3150
                                                                        CIP

ISBN 1-888602-08-2

To Linda, Karen, Lauren, and Mark

What becomes of that sacred thing, friendship, if even the friend is not loved for his (or her) own sake . . . ? Why, according to this theory, a friend should even be deserted and cast aside as soon as there is no longer hope of benefit and profit from his (or her) friendship! But what could be more inhuman than that?

Cicero, *On the Laws*

Contents

Preface

This is the story of C. G. Jung's friendships with Mary
Mellon and J. B. Priestley, friendships that led to greater
awareness of Jung's psychology in America and Britain.
I believe that Jung's friendship with Mary Mellon has a
number of historical significances. First, it sheds further
light on both people, and their humanity. Franz Jung
told me that his father had "a nose and ears"—that he
was human.[1] It is a C. G. Jung with "a nose and ears"
who appears in the correspondence with Mary Mellon.
Secondly, Jung's letters tell what it felt like to live in
Switzerland during World War II; they clearly show that
he was anti-Nazi during the War. His friendship with
Mellon, moreover, eventually led to a greater awareness
of his psychology in the United States and Great Britain,
through the translation and publication of his works. Finally, it illustrates a psychological dimension to the
support of ideas. Philanthropic or other support for ideas
does not occur in a vacuum—it involves psychological
motivations and factors. The psychological dimension
may be less striking in other instances than in the case
at hand, but historians must nevertheless recognize that
it exists.

In 1946—the same year that Mary Mellon died—
Jung's friendship with J. B. Priestley began. Priestley did
a BBC broadcast on Jung and his work; when Jung saw
the transcript he commented that he had never seen a
better summary of his main ideas in such a concise
form—he called it a masterpiece. Later in 1946, Priestley persuaded Jung to do a talk for the BBC: "The Fight
with the Shadow." In 1954, when Jung was about to publish his *Answer to Job* in Britain—which his publishers
in America had not dared to print, Priestley wrote two
articles supporting and defending Jung's works, for
which Jung was very grateful. *Journey Down a Rainbow*,
by Priestley and Jacquetta Hawkes, was the last book
Emma Jung read before her death in 1955.

The historian must have sufficient historical evidence
and be wary of psychological reductionism. I am grateful to the heirs of Jung for permitting me to examine
Jung's letters to Mary Mellon and the Jung-Priestley correspondence in the Jung Archives. I am equally thankful
to Paul Mellon for permitting me to examine Mary's letters to Jung. Dr. Beat Glaus and his courteous staff at the
Jung Archives, Swiss Federal Institute of Technology Library, Zurich, provided me with the manuscripts on an
almost daily basis for a number of months. Eric N.
Lindquist, at Paul Mellon's office in Washington, D.C.,
kindly provided pertinent materials, too. Michigan State
University gave me a Global Competence grant and two
leaves of absence that enabled me to do research in
Zurich. The Harry Ransom Humanities Research Center, University of Texas at Austin, permitted me access
to those three letters from Jung to Priestley in its J. B.
Priestley Collection that were not represented at the
Jung Archives. Edward McInnis and Kim Lyerly, my re-

search assistants at Michigan State University and the University of Texas respectively, helpfully and ably performed research tasks. Fred Bauman, of the Manuscript Division of the Library of Congress, Washington, D.C., rendered assistance that let me determine that all copies of C. G. Jung-Mary Mellon letters and cables in the Bollingen Foundation Papers deposited there were at the Jung Archives as well. Under a Freedom of Information Act request, the Federal Bureau of Investigation, Washington, D.C., let me examine copies of the FBI reports on Jung. The British Broadcasting Corporation Written Archives Centre, Reading, Berkshire, let me see the script of Priestley's broadcast talk on Jung. To all of the above I am grateful. I wish to say a special word of thanks to my wife, Linda, for being my traveling companion during research overseas and here, and to Jake Foglio for his encouragement of this work.

Note:

1. Interview with Franz Jung, May 22, 1991.

Acknowledgments

I gratefully acknowledge the permission of Paul Mellon to quote letters by Mary Mellon to C. G. Jung, August 26, 1941 (together with the enclosure dated August 14, 1941), November 26, 1941, and November 10, 1945, and of Niedieck Linder AG—literary agency for the Jung heirs—to quote Jung to Mary Mellon, September 24, 1945 and to J. B. Priestley, July 17, 1946 and January 27, 1950.

I am thankful for permission to quote Jung to Mary Mellon, April 18, 1941 and to Priestley, July 17, 1946 and November 8, 1954, published in Jung, C. G., *Letters*, ed. Gerhard Adler and Aniela Jaffé, volumes 1-2, © 1971, 1973; 1975 by Princeton University Press and Routledge (London). Reprinted by permission of Princeton University Press and Routledge.

Part I

C. G. Jung and Mary Mellon

There were days when the sun bathed the variously storied white and pastel houses steeply perched on the hillsides overlooking the lake, and sparkled on the waters below as her auto sped from Zurich to Küsnacht. Here she drove past old stuccoed houses with weathered red-tiled roofs and small fenced gardens to the more spacious white house of C. G. Jung, on the lake where he lived and had his practice. She was beginning sessions with him. It was autumn, 1939. War had already broken out. Nazi German airplanes and tanks had been loosed on Poland by their psychologically misshapen master. I shall try to tell the story of the friendship of Jung and Mary Mellon, of her generous support of his psychology, and of other matters of historical interest that appear in their correspondence.

In December, 1933, Paul Mellon met Mary Conover Brown, daughter of a Kansas City specialist in internal medicine. She was striking in appearance, outgoing, impulsively enthusiastic, easy to talk to, and interested in all sorts of things. When Paul later met her parents he found Charles Conover to be a highly intelligent and

nice man; he found Perla Petty Conover pretty negative. Mary had suffered attacks of asthma since childhood. Realizing that they might have a psychosomatic
element, Dr. Conover had studied it and from time to
time attempted to treat her.[1]

Paul, the son of Andrew W. Mellon—one of the
wealthiest persons in the United States and former Secretary of the Treasury—knew he wanted to marry her
from the moment they met. She was recently divorced
from her husband of four years, Karl Stanley Brown. She
was a graduate of Vassar, class of 1926; Paul was a graduate of Yale, 1929. Within four or five months after
they met they became engaged. They married in February, 1935.[2]

In 1934, Mary and Paul both read Jung's *Modern Man
in Search of a Soul*, with which they were impressed.
While Mary had suffered from asthma since childhood,
Paul had suffered from his parents' mismatched marriage, and their separation and divorce. In New York,
Mary and Paul began consulting Ann Moyer, who they
were told was a Jungian analyst.[3] In February, 1936,
while they were staying in England at Bibury Court,
Cirencester, Gloucestershire, Mary wrote to Jung for
the first time. She had asked the advice of Ann Moyer—
now Moyer van Waveren—about consulting Jung, and
Moyer van Waveren had advised it most strongly. Mary
informed Jung that she had worked with her analyst for
over a year. She asked whether it would be possible to
see him, how much time Jung could give her over a period of a month, and what his fees were. Thus began the
Mellon-Jung correspondence.[4]

It was not possible for Mary to see Jung at this time.
The Mellons did see Jung, however, in October, 1937, at
a seminar on "Dream Symbols and the Individuation

Process" that Jung gave under the auspices of the Analytical Psychology Club in New York—after he had delivered his Terry Lectures on "Religion in the Light of Science and Philosophy" at Yale. Though the Mellons were not yet well enough acquainted with Jung's ideas really to understand his seminar, they were deeply impressed with him. In December, 1937, Paul Mellon wrote to Jung. He told Jung that Mary and he had been working with Moyer van Waveren for three years and that, through her, they had attended his seminar in New York. Both were eager to attend his seminar in Zurich during May and June 1938. Paul asked whether that were possible and also asked Jung for as little, or as much, time as he could give them individually. Paul requested an answer at the earliest opportunity, since the couple wanted to make plans for living in Zurich.[5]

On December 16, Jung's secretary replied that they could attend the seminar in May and June, though it would probably be impossible for them to see Jung individually. Paul informed the secretary that they definitely intended to come to the seminar.[6] In March, 1938, the Mellons set off for Europe from their farm, Rokeby, in Upperville, Virginia, with their one-year-old daughter, Cathy. They stayed in London *en route* to Zurich. From Claridge's in Brook Street, Paul asked Jung's secretary whether he could work with Toni Wolff, Jung's closest associate, during their stay.[7]

The Mellons set out for Zurich on May 6, and remained in Switzerland for eight weeks. They attended Jung's seminar in English on the subject of Friedrich Nietzsche's *Thus Spake Zarathustra*. After the seminar and toward the end of their stay, they drove down to Ascona on beautiful Lake Maggiore in Italian-speaking southern Switzerland. Jung happened to be on holiday in Ascona and they saw him individually on their last day. They then returned to the United States from Bremerhaven, Germany, on the *Europa*. They planned to return to Switzerland later in summer of the following year—1939—to attend the Eranos conference at Ascona.[8]

In July, 1939, the Mellons returned to Europe by sailing from New York to Genoa, Italy. From there, they drove up into the mountains to Ascona and arrived on July 31. The conference started on August 7. On most days of the conference, Olga Froebe-Kapteyn, its hostess, invited them for luncheon at a large round table on the terrace of Casa Gabriella, her house on Lake Maggiore. On August 9 and 11 they each had an appointment with Jung at which it was arranged that each would work with him individually over the coming months. After the conference ended on August 28, the couple motored up to Zurich, initially staying at the Dolder Grand Hotel in the hills above the city. Soon they took an apartment at 68 Plattenstrasse, near the Psychological Club where Jung held his seminars. Both started working individually with him at the end of September. Mary even went to his lectures in German at the Federal Institute of Technology, where Jung taught.[9]

From the Mellons' apartment it was only about a ten-minute walk to the Federal Institute of Technology. From its terrace Mary could see Zurich displaying its charms before her: to the left, toward the lake, the Grossmünster with its large twin towers; across the River Limmat, the Fraumünster with its tall green steeple; to its right, St. Peter's Church with—it was said—the biggest clock in Europe; and in the foreground, the *Predigerkirche* (Preachers' Church).

When Hitler attacked Poland on September 1, 1939, Jung at first thought Mary had left Europe. When he realized she had remained, he wrote her that it was courageous to stay and share whatever fate had in store for them. He recommended Dr. Eleanor Bertine as a possible analyst if she did return to the States—he had heard that she had disagreed with the van Waverens. As it turned out, Mary remained in Europe for the next eight months, and Jung was her analyst. This letter in early September of 1939 is signed: Sincerely yours.[10]

As the analysis proceeded, a strong transference and countertransference developed between Mary and Jung. The growing strength of the transference and countertransference can be seen in the quality of the subsequent correspondence and in the signatures. In December, Mary sent Jung a picture of himself and one of Ascona that Paul had taken. She teased that she could just hear him laugh: Did she look like a wet mouse the day of the party? Did he feel like a caged lion? She mentioned that the Mellons were going to Arosa on the next day, and would be at the Kulm Hotel should he have time to write.[11]

In April, Jung wrote to Mary from Ascona while he was on holiday. Mary had undergone an emergency operation for appendicitis in Zurich. While she was convalescing, Paul had joined Jung on a walking holiday in the mountains near Locarno.[12] Jung observed that Paul had seemed to enjoy the walks and the beautiful weather in the Italian-speaking south of Switzerland. Jung said Mary was "an angel" to think of him in his present mentally tired conditions—where idly looking at pictures was a welcome relaxation. He thanked her for the books she had also sent, and said that she was really too nice and too generous. He mentioned "a hell" of a trick her Christian name Mary played with him, as he was thinking of Gnostic texts and the name Maria. He hoped that she would soon be getting stronger. The letter is signed more warmly: Cordially.[13]

In April of 1940, the War—which had been quiet during the winter—erupted. Denmark and Norway were invaded; German forces prepared to invade the Low Countries and France as well. The Mellons made arrangements to return to the United States.

Lastly, on the afternoon of April 29, they went to tea at Jung's retreat in a secluded natural setting near the village of Bollingen on the Upper Lake of Zurich.[14] Across the lake, green hills rose toward Alpine peaks in the distance. In this setting, amidst solitude and nature, it was doubtless easy for Mary to see the man not only as her analyst but also as a modern prophet who had things of value to teach. Mary subsequently gave the name Bollingen to the idea that she conceived for the translation and publication of Jung's works in English.

The Mellons set sail for the United States: Mary with their daughter on May 3 from Genoa, and Paul two weeks later after closing up their apartment on Plattenstrasse. Fearing that communications with America would be cut off, Jung wrote in haste on June 19. He thought that night had descended on Europe and that only one certainty remained: nothing could put out the light within. He wished her and Paul every good wish and signed the letter a warmer "affectionately."[15]

Responding to Mary's telegram on his birthday, July 26, Jung gave his perception of conditions in Switzerland and in Europe. He wrote that the Swiss government had advised people to lay in stores of food: Switzerland could support itself if its people would eat one-fifth less. No shortage of milk and meat would occur unless Germany invaded and robbed Switzerland. The Swiss remained afraid that Germany would destroy them. Germany might not benefit, Jung noted, but reason was not the criterion by which the present German mentality could be understood. It was thoroughly irrational and mystical—a mistaken quest for the eternal kingdom on earth. People like that were miserable and they spread misery. In contrast, Jung was convinced that a kingdom could not be conquered somewhere on the map of Europe, but only within. Turning to other subjects Jung mentioned that, though he had no intention to speak at the recent Eranos conference at Ascona, he did speak on the psychology of the three Persons of the Trinity. Then it took him ten full days afterwards to work out all the improvident things he had blurted out at the meeting. Jung said it would be too nice for words if one could kiss her helpful hand—Hélas—Vous êtes trop loin! Returning to the subject of the War, he remarked that France had been completely rotten. He had seen a good number of the French interned in Switzerland, and said it was a complete moral crash on the part of France. He concluded by saying that Europeans were now in prison: God save our souls. That was more important than butter![16] In response to a gift of records of black spirituals that Mary had sent, a subsequent letter from Jung added the observation that it was too bad the world suffered from Nazi Germany's outburst of insanity. Jung judged that it would suspend every reasonable communication—presumably for years.[17]

In response to the beautiful camellia Mary sent to him at Christmas, Jung mentioned that several times she appeared to him quite vividly. Germany's war against Britain, and the destruction of France, he said, were almost more than one could bear. The devastation of London by bombing had hurt Jung as if England were his own country. Her plans for an enclosed garden at the Mellon house—something not only in the mind but in earth and stone—gave him a feeling of peace and restfulness, something to look forward to beyond the abomination of war and Germany's Nietzschean insanity. Jung continued, saying it was now a question whether they in Europe could retain the treasures of culture against the onslaught of the powers of darkness. In Switzerland, he remarked, everything was as if frozen. People still moved about and trains ran, but automobiles had almost vanished from streets. Food was still plentiful, but everything cost more. The army concentrated in the Alps in the event of invasion, but the lower country in Switzerland would have to be sacrificed. It would be madness to attack Switzerland, said Jung, but the Germans were mad. All the Swiss sympathies were on the British side.

The news Jung received from Germany was contradictory. A well-informed German told him that about ninety percent were against the regime. A Swiss from Berlin mentioned that workmen criticized Hitler and called him a liar. But the young people in Germany were still full of illusions, though the mood in the army had dropped since Britain could not be conquered. People from Paris told Jung that the Germans were unlikely to succeed in administering the conquered countries, since they lacked enough qualified personnel. Jung stated that he did not dare send Mary his recent paper, "Das göttliche Kind"—produced with Professor Karl Kerényi—for fear it would get lost. Parcels were still unsafe, and communications might cease altogether. Perhaps Switzerland would fall under German domination. In that case he would certainly be silenced;

he would not mind, provided he still had his books and a roof over his head. But he hoped to see her again and sent her every good wish.[18]

In February, Mary wrote Marie-Jeanne Schmid, Jung's secretary, to request a list of the books in English in Jung's library. Before the Mellons had left for the United States, Jung had told her she could take down the names of these books, but she had been very rushed and had not had time to make the list. Most of the books on Jung's shelves had to be ordered from England, Mary thought, and she would like to order them while communications were still open.[19] Schmid made the list and sent it to Mary, though with probably unintended humor she noted it contained a lot of uninteresting books—especially among the psychological ones. She observed that almost the greater part of the books on the list had been printed in the United States.[20]

Subsequent correspondence in 1941 shows that Mary was becoming too much identified with Jung: it was showing in her dreams. In April, Jung responded to dreams about "twin children, twin men, twin Jungs." These dreams suggested the projection of a dualism in her that became chiefly visible in him. Jung said it was probable that it should be seen in him rather than in her. It was a dualism in the unconscious (therefore projected) personality for which he was the paradigm in her dream. The idea could be formulated in the well-known Hindu style: he was yea and nay. His invitation meant that she should come up to the level of such understanding, "whose vehicle is love and not the mind. This love is not transference and it is no ordinary friendship or sympathy. It is more primitive, more primeval and more spiritual, than anything we can describe. That upper floor is no more you or I, it means many, including yourself and anybody whose heart you touch. There is no distance, but immediate presence. It is an eternal secret, how shall I ever explain it?"[21]

On Jung's birthday, he received a message from Paul and from Mary. Paul had joined the United States Army and he was presently in the cavalry. He was completely satisfied that it was his place and it would be an invaluable experience. She also sent her own best wishes and signed the telegram: All love, Mary Mellon.[22]

A very significant letter from Mary a month later announced a disconcerting dream about Jung. Mary had never had one like it before where he was concerned, and it had much distressed her. She asked him to tell her how he felt about it and what he thought it meant. She gave an account of the dream, dated August 14, in an enclosure accompanying the letter.[23]

DREAM

August 14, 1941

I was with Jung in a foreign place. Had something to do with the war. Jung had changed in appearance. He had got leaner and harder and his hair was Prussian looking. He still loved me, but apparently I was a source for some kind of information all of which was found in the past correspondence of Jung and myself. These were the things Jung was betraying me with. I had the letters in my possession and trusting him completely I gave him everything he asked for. It was a most complete betrayal, yet I knew he loved me and also that he was possessed. I could see by the different look in his eye . . . hurried and greedy.

Then I finally found out and confronted him with the betrayal. He had gone so far that he had to go on, but for an instant he changed and the old look came into his eyes and he took me in his arms. I said "This is not the Jung who wrote the green letters to me". (Those letters he did not want back or use in the scheme). He knew he was possessed too.

Somehow I knew that if Miss Wolff [Toni Wolff, Jung's colleague and intimate friend] were there everything would be alright. He had always told me of the devil in every man and I was seeing his. It would be exorcised by Miss Wolff. After he finished loving me his face changed again and he went on with his work. I was so very sad and hopeless, because I believed in him still.

Then the dream changed.

I was driving an old broken down car past Paul who was playing some game in a field. The car had manure on the back of it. Man Paul was playing with said it was I but Paul said no it couldn't be. He said I wouldn't drive that car, that anyway it was economically impossible. I left the car and ran quickly up to my room. Mother and the maids were there. It was as if I were hiding and this some plot. I saw Paul go up to the car, still denying it could be I.[24]

Mary's letter contained still other significant items besides the dream.

I simply do not know what to make of this dream. I have never had one like it before, where you were concerned. I have pondered and pondered it. Am I in some way betraying myself? Has my Self changed so completely? It has distressed me so much and I get nowhere. Am I overestimating you consciously so that I must have this compensating kind of dream, or what? Oh, if I could only *talk* to you again. Will you write and tell me how you feel about it and what you think it means?

It is six weeks now since Paul left to join the Army and it has been a queer time for me. First of all I never knew how much I loved him I guess, until he really went somewhere completely out of reach, where neither he nor I could do anything about it. It is the first time we have had this kind of thing happen, because before we could always arrange somehow, no matter what the circumstances. That is one of the good things about it I think. But it is very lonely without him. I don't suppose you have heard from him yet, because he has had little or no time to write to anyone. He tells me that he has never before felt so well, or looked so well. He has turned out to be a marvelous shot, which amazed him and everyone else and I believe [he] will go a long way in the Army. He says that he is terribly glad that he took the step.

I heard from Frau Frobe that the Tagung [Eranos Conference] was a great success and that your lecture [on Transformation Symbolism in the Mass] was wonderful. She cabled, asking me if I would publish it! Really. Isn't *that* wonderful? I replied very formally that I would be glad to and to send the manuscript at once. Your eyes are laughing at me this very moment in the picture in front of me.

The Mellons had begun the Bollingen Press in late 1940:

The Press is going forward slowly, as it should. I have got Mrs. Baynes to say that she would let me publish the I Ging after the Eranos book, then will come yours. I think that makes a very good beginning. Zimmer will probably contribute something after that, and I have found a little 16th century book in French on Alchemy which I want to translate and reprint. It is written by "Un Amateur de la Verite".

Mary knew some persons among whom "there is such a longing, Dr. Jung [as she nearly always addressed him], to know what is the matter, so to speak, with themselves and what they are doing and why, when they approach everything with reason, it turns out so badly all the time." She went on to tell Jung about life in the United States in 1941:

Life goes on pretty much as usual except for the growing war feeling in this country. At least growing talk of war. The meeting of Churchill and Roosevelt in the Atlantic [to formulate the Atlantic Charter] had a great effect, but as I told you before the country is so split that it would not surprise me to see a Civil War, before we get into the big one. Names have been given the two sides. You are either an Isolationist or an Interventionist. I am an Interventionist, but it doesn't seem to do much good. The magic word has not been spoken yet in this country. There is tremendous apathy about the whole thing and the labor situation is dreadful, what with strikes in almost every defense plant etc. In the minds of the people the Atlantic is still so broad and the rest of the world so far away. I believe nothing short of invasion will bring people to their senses and then we shall be in for it. [Later in 1941, Pearl Harbor would show her to be correct.] Russia has held out wonderfully, hasn't she? but I don't know how long she will last. It is a sad state of affairs all the way round.

I am still busy building the house and doing my garden. I have not joined any Volunteer Service yet, because I think it is more important to keep this community in order so far than to be running around in a uniform, taking motors to pieces and folding bandages. There are so many women who adore uniforms and bandages. Since Paul is away I have a great deal more responsibility to the people who are working here, and I shall stick to that.

Sometimes I have a strong feeling that you would like to see me as much as I want to see you. I wonder if that is true. Then it fades away. Tell me if you ever do because it would help me to know it sometimes. Anyway the grass is green and the fire still burns.

She signed the letter: All my love to you, Mary.[25] The letter and the dream together indicate that in her transference Mary projected images of father, lover, and modern prophet on Jung. In Jungian terms this appears to be a classical animus transference.

Some of Jung's words in his previous letter of April 18 and now in his reply of September 8 may have had the unintentional effect of encouraging Mary to identify too much with him. That he sometimes flirted with her— and by implication other women—seems obvious from the letters. He told her he often thought of her and he often wished he could see her again. But she was further away than the moon. He thought of her in Ascona, where they had a nice conference. Her dream, he said, was indeed shocking. She got such a dream when she was too much identified with somebody. The unconscious then attempted to throw something in between. Jung suggested that Mary probably had a living image of him and it might keep her too much away from herself, no matter what he was. It must be something of the kind, for all her letters emanated an immediate warmth and something like a living substance that had an almost compelling effect. He got emotional about them and could do something foolish if she were not on the other side of the Atlantic. He asked her not to misunderstand him: he was in a healthy condition of mind but he merely described, with utmost honesty, the effect of a letter of hers. There was a living connection through the non-space, an unconscious identity. It was dangerous to a certain degree, for it could cause a certain alienation from herself. He considered her dream a very necessary compensation, though painful. His attitude was one of honest and sincere devotion beyond doubt. It had never changed. She needed to do nothing about it, since he thought a normally functioning unconscious would compensate the trouble efficiently. It was—for example—sufficient to get this shock of a poisonous dream. Jung further pointed out that they had to realize that no matter how much they would like to talk they would be separated for a long time, maybe forever. She ought, he said, to realize the facts as they were. In Switzerland, they did not know what was going to happen. Germany exhaled a devastating atmosphere. He asked her to give his best regards to Paul and signed the letter: Affectionately.[26]

In October, Mary was startled by a cable from Jung

that read simply: No nonsense about Zosimos.[27] Mary replied that she was bewildered by his cable. Subsequently, she telephoned Ximena de Angulo, her assistant editor at the Bollingen Press; she found that Ximena had sent a few changes in Jung's manuscript on Zosimos of Panopolis that Mary had okayed, and an introductory note that Mary had not seen and Ximena had no right to send. The manuscript was among the manuscripts for the projected Eranos volume. Mary assumed this was the nonsense of which Jung spoke. Mary had forcibly corrected Ximena and there would be no further nonsense unless it were Mary's own. She signed the cable: All love, Mary Mellon.[28] By cable Jung replied that Ximena's changes were unimportant. Barbara Hannah had pestered him about them. There was no worry.[29] A letter from Jung explained the situation further. He apologized if he had disturbed Mary by his impetuous telegram. He had become somewhat irritated by Barbara Hannah's complaints about Ximena's changes in the Zosimos manuscript. It would be best if the new English text were left as it was. Certain Greek words in the text should not be eliminated as they contributed to understanding its meaning. The letter went on to say that Frau Froebe-Kapteyn wished to collect for the Eranos archive a vast number of ancient and medieval pictures of Hermes—a decidedly useful enterprise. But she needed some money to pay for the necessary photos. Hermes was the main subject of the next Eranos Conference. The Eranos enterprise had only private supporters and, for the time being, it was impossible to raise more money in Switzerland. Jung contributed his collaboration and $250 annually, but that was all he could do. Switzerland had very few people who could give something. There were plenty of wealthy people in Switzerland but, said Jung, they did not care. Jung was so very much obliged to Mary Mellon for her generous interest in his humble efforts to do something for the spiritual welfare of this "godforsaken" world that he hated to bother her for such trifles. He concluded by saying that he hoped she did not allow life to become too complicated. It is better when it is simple. Jung also said that he had reduced his work with patients, and had given up public lectures. He confined himself to scientific work. He hoped his last letter had reached her.[30]

Mary's reply on November 26 was handwritten and three-and-a-half pages long. First, she was upset that apparently one of his letters had been lost.

> I'm very much upset that one of your letters has been lost—I have too few of them in the first place without the British Empire taking liberties. I know of no way to retrieve it either. I wonder if any of mine have gone astray. You never answer specifically so it is hard to tell—except about the dreams—when they are too much to overlook.
>
> The one about your betraying me was a terrible shock—and I know I needed it in just that fashion. Cathy, who is a barometer for me, said just about that time—on looking at the snake medallion on my wrist—"I'm tired of that one—why don't you wear the other" (meaning the clover Paul had given me) that set me thinking and coupled with the dream I had an inkling that something of the sort, which you told me in your letter, was wrong. Then you explained it.
>
> But it is so hard, Dr. Jung, to be so connected and not run into such pitfalls. I can't help the former and it takes eternal vigilance to be aware of the danger of losing myself in you.

Mary went on to say:

But the opposite is true too. I look back now on the two years since I have seen you of your feeling for me. Paradoxically, that is what left me free to be myself and really love you.

I know, as well as you, that we may never see one another again, but after your last letter I feel better about it. I begin to see just why not seeing you again could never alter anything, though at the same time there is nothing I want more—and perhaps we shall. The whole thing is so strange that it may contain that too.

All these realizations about myself in connection with you are the sole cause, I am sure, of my being able to conceive another child—which has just happened. No one else would believe or understand—nor does anyone else have to—but it is true.

It is a strange thing—the feeling of being with child again—and stranger still to know and, though it doesn't sound like very much—a good deal has happened *through* you, but not *of* you—so to speak—if you understand what I mean. I know that everything is the result of the miraculous year I spent with you—but one thing leads me to believe that I have kept or gained my own identity. That is the difference there is between my expression and that of those around me who have also been touched by you.

In other words there are people who live and breathe Jung, as you know. It is a pattern they take up—based on your ways, your likes and dislikes, your mode of living, speech—and to my great amazement—even handwriting. I have had letters from one or two in the N.Y. Psychological Club—and I swear I had to look twice to see if it weren't yours.

I am sure I would have fallen into the same pattern had it not been for the realization or feel [sic] what connection it has with what has happened to me these past three years.

Then Mary told Jung:

I express it badly but somehow, somewhere, someway—you are in this child too. It is as if I had been twice impregnated, for had it not been for the brutal and spiritual anguish which you and I have forced me to go through, I do not believe I would ever have conceived again.

> I would never have got to the place where I knew what
> Paul is—who I am in relation to him, what I must be in rela-
> tion to the world—and what I am in relation to you. It all
> came to me in a wave the night of October 7—and I wrote
> Paul a letter. This child was conceived soon after.
> It is all so strange and mysterious—so very difficult and
> marvelous—that I am baffled and can only thank God that I
> understand even a slight part of it. 37 years ago, you once told
> me, you began to analyse—37 years ago I was born. I don't un-
> derstand.

In conclusion, she told him that she would write another letter—typewritten and business-like—about the
Bollingen Press:

> I'm writing another letter Friday about the Press. It will be
> typewritten and business like—I have lots to ask you.
> I've sent you two little books for Christmas. I think they
> are both charming. I hope you like them. The other two, in
> Latin, you may or may not have—one is about dreams and
> the other *laughing*. Tell me what you think of them.
> Please write as soon as you can.

She signed the letter: With all my love to you, Dr. Jung,
Mary.[31]

The cooler tone of Jung's reply indicates that he
wanted to encourage no further overidentification with
him. He thanked Mary for the Christmas presents of
flowers, books, and provisions. Jung said that in his letters he had not (except for dreams) referred to the contents of her previous letters because of the interval between letters and because he sometimes got mixed up
between two letters. Such a din existed in the world
that one experienced the greatest difficulty in holding
his mind decently together. He had a quiet winter except for the "grippe" but he was beginning to pick up
again slowly. He supposed Paul was now with the

army: He had always had the impression that Paul had the psychology of someone waiting to be picked up by something not yet in sight. Even if Jung did not refer to her letters, he read them very carefully and they were registered. He was looking forward to another letter because he liked to hear from the other side of the Atlantic. The European condition was indescribable, at least as it was experienced in Switzerland. Hellish suspense existed. Everything was provisional; life moved forward like the ticking of a clock which may not be wound again. He hoped that she was in good health despite the rush of a country now in war, and he signed the letter: I remain, yours cordially, C. G. Jung.[32]

In February, Mary finished the typewritten and business-like letter about the Bollingen Press that she had promised. She began on a personal note: Mrs. Cabot had just sent her some new pictures of Jung and Toni Wolff that had made Mary so homesick she could scarcely bear it. World events seemed to be separating them more and more. The realization of a long war had finally dawned on America she said. The Atlantic was not safely passable, and she was afraid that even mail communications might be stopped. She was hurrying to send the letter so that Jung could respond at the earliest date. Then Mary turned to business. The Bollingen Press had become the Bollingen Foundation for the same purpose but this seemed a better way of doing it. They were now free to choose whatever publishing house they liked. They had intended, first of all, to publish the collection of essays from Eranos conferences. These essays had all been translated and readied to print, but the Board (consisting of Heinrich Zimmer, Edgar Wind, Stringfellow Barr, Cary Baynes, Ximena de Angulo, and Mary) decided that the collection was too disjointed to be their first book. They all thought it wiser to publish a subsequent collection of Eranos essays from one year with one theme. Mary commented that it was taking far longer to start a new venture like Bollingen than she had anticipated. What Mary really wanted to discuss with Jung was the question of translating and publishing his books in English.[33]

Mary put forward a very coherent outline of six points—the first explicit proposal to publish Jung's collected works. Point (1): Mary suggested that they publish Jung's work on the *Mass*, which Cary Baynes was translating. Alternatively, they might publish it in conjunction with Father Jud's lectures on the Mass given at the Psychological Club of Zurich. She asked for his opinion. Point (2): Since they had abandoned the collection of Eranos essays, it left hanging his essay on Zosimos. She would rather wait, however long, until he had finished a book on Alchemy and have Zosimos appear as a part of it—rather than as a bit and piece beforehand. Point (3): She envisioned publishing all his works in a beautiful, substantial, uniform edition, bit by bit, so that people could get at them. It could be done over time. She suggested that they begin with the *Two Essays on Analytical Psychology*—which were out of print and very difficult to obtain—and the *Psychology of the Unconscious*—which was also out of print and badly needed a new translation. Point (4): They could start translating the *Göttliche Kind* right away and publish it within the year. Point (5): If he approved, she would love to publish the *VII Sermones ad Mortuos* in a beautiful leather binding. It was wonderful and she had reread it many times. Of course, if he wished, no one need know it was his—it could be published pseudonymously. Point (6): He could make any number of suggestions to her about works in German that could be translated or about reprints. She asked him to respond and tell her in outline form how he felt about the six points and also to give her his conception of how to go about publishing his writings, the order in which they should appear, and any suggestions he might have.[34]

Mary had founded the Bollingen Press with Jung as the keystone and for the purpose of disseminating his teaching as her contribution to his work. She said it was important to her to have his ideas on his books. She wanted the series to be a substantial one, and she wanted to make no mistakes so far as he was concerned. The world seemed in such a mess that it became all the more important to her to do what she could to keep alive and make available his works and other real, scholarly, and imaginative books on human beings and the history of the human soul. It was all she could do and she wanted to do it well. She enclosed a list of the books that they had at hand or that were in the offing for possible publication. The tentative list of publications, as it was headed, included twelve works. Four were by Jung, one by Emma Jung, and one by Toni Wolff: Jung's *Transformation Symbolism of the Mass*, *Two Essays* (reprint), *Psychology of the Unconscious* (new edition, translated), and, under the pseudonym Basilides, *VII Sermones ad Mortuos*, Emma Jung's *Grail*, and—Mary also hoped—a book of essays from Toni Wolff. The other six works were: Richard Wilhelm, *I Ching* (translated from the German by Cary Baynes); Andrew Gibb, *In Search of Sanity*; Hans Leisegang, *The Serpent Mystery*; William Troy, *Orpheus: The Artist as Scapegoat*; Ernesto Buonaiuti,

Love and Death in the Greek Tragic Poets; and Heinrich Zimmer, *Manual of Hindu Art.*[35]
Jung replied in detail to the proposal. He said that her letter of February 20 had not arrived until early April and it had been forwarded to him at Bollingen, where he was on holiday. He was impressed with the change from the Bollingen Press to the Bollingen Foundation, and he was glad, too, that Mary had changed the original idea of publishing first a collection of essays from Eranos Conferences. He then responded to Mary's six points one by one. (1): He advised her to wait to publish his "Mass," for he was improving the manuscript. It was now independent from Father Jud's lectures, and it could be published with or without Jud's historical description of the Mass. (2): He advised her not to publish "Zosimos" as a monograph, for it really belonged to the series of alchemical researches. She was right in wanting to wait until she could get it in its proper place. (3): If she wanted to publish the *Two Essays* he advised her to wait until he sent her the manuscript of the new revised edition of the "Unconscious in the Normal and Pathological Mind" which he was now preparing. The other essay, "The Relation of the Ego to the Unconscious," could do without revision. Moreover, the *Psychology of the Unconscious* badly needed a new translation, but he would like to produce a revised German manuscript first, for a number of things needed improvement. (4): Dr. K. W. Bash was already translating the "Göttliche Kind" in Zurich. He pointed out that there had been transactions with Routledge, but that nothing was settled. It might solve difficulties, Jung said, if she published it using Bash's translation. He could look over the translation before it was printed. (5): He advised her to wait regarding the "Seven Ser-

mones." He had contemplated adding certain materials but he had hesitated for years to do it. Still, he might risk it. (6): He was grateful for her permission to make suggestions about other publications and translations. He suggested that she might choose the actual German edition of his papers. He was preparing two volumes. The first consisted of a new edition of the "Dream Symbols of the Individuation Process" and "Ideas of Redemption in Alchemy." The second volume contained "Zosimos," the "Mass," the "Trinity," and Marie Louise von Franz's "Passio Perpetuae" (Passion of St. Perpetua). The difficulty about the first volume would be that the two papers were contained in *Integration of the Personality* published by Farrar and Rinehart, but perhaps Mary had already considered it. As to the second volume, Jung asked if he could glance through the English translations before publication.[36]

All in all, Jung gave a positive and encouraging response to Mary's proposal to publish his works in English. Having responded to her detailed outline of six points he suggested, on the whole, the publication of the simpler things first: the *Two Essays on Analytical Psychology* and the *Psychology of the Unconscious*. He would send the revised manuscripts to her as soon as possible. He added that he was planning a third volume of papers in German. It consisted of papers on archetypes, but he thought it best to publish none of these papers separately as monographs since they belonged together—and made sense only together. In conclusion, Jung turned to the War. His family was beginning to feel the restrictions of rationing. Only bread, vegetables, fruit, wine, and tobacco were not yet rationed. The winter had been long and cold; even the potatoes in the cellar froze, but they were edible. Perhaps in the near future all communications with America would be cut. The condition of Europe became worse every day: the misery in the occupied countries was indescribable. The air vibrated with lies and rumors, and it was almost impossible to tell true from false information. He signed the letter: I remain yours gratefully.[37]

Jung was very surprised to receive a stiff, formal letter over Mary's signature informing him that, due to the war emergency and restrictions placed on American citizens in their relations with persons abroad, the Bollingen Foundation had decided to cease all activities abroad, particularly in Switzerland. Her lawyer, Donald Shepard, had drafted the letter.[38] In it, Mary informed Jung that the U.S. Government had put into effect a Trading with the Enemy Act that had drastic provisions against American citizens dealing with enemy aliens, directly or even *indirectly*. Consequently, the Foundation decided that its activities during the War should be restricted—particularly with regard to receiving manuscripts and material from abroad for publication. It further decided to discontinue all activities abroad, including correspondence and financial aid such as had been rendered to Olga Froebe-Kapteyn at Ascona (who had wrongly come under suspicion by the Federal Bureau of Investigation). No member of the Foundation desired to have any dealings with an enemy alien, directly or indirectly. Consequently, Paul and she felt that it was desirable to cease all activities in Switzerland. Only in this way could they be sure they might not be directly or indirectly coming into contact with an enemy alien. She regretted very much the necessity of this course of action but above all they wished in no way, albeit unwittingly, to do anything that might render assistance to the enemy or be subject to criticism. Until the War ended they would confine the Foundation's activities to manuscripts and materials in the United States. She hoped Jung was well and sent her kind regards.[39]

In July, a formal letter from Donald Shepard informed Jung that the functioning of the Bollingen Foundation during the War had been further considered and it had been decided to cease all activities whatsoever. The Foundation, therefore, had been completely liquidated and dissolved—it was now out of existence. Shepard further said Mrs. Mellon was very disappointed that circumstances necessitated stopping what she considered a much-needed and worthwhile work and, particularly, the delay that would be occasioned in the publication of Jung's works in English. She would maintain a deep interest in the project and, following the end of the War and when circumstances permitted, she would revive the Foundation so that Jung's work as outlined in his letter of April 10 might be carried forward immediately. She hoped that he would reserve publication of those items until her Foundation could function once more.[40]

On the occasion of Jung's birthday, Mary and Paul Mellon sent him a telegram wishing him a very happy birthday and informing him that they had a son born to them and named Timothy. The telegram was signed "love."[41]

Jung formally replied to Shepard's letter informing him of the dissolution of the Bollingen Foundation. He regretted to hear that the Fund had been dissolved, but he appreciated the urgency of the reasons for the decision. He requested that his best regards be given to Mr. and Mrs. Paul Mellon.[42] Though Jung did not say so to Mary, friends of his in Zurich told Cary Baynes in later years about his resentment of the cold letters.[43]

In early 1943, however, the Bollingen idea was revived. In February, Heinrich Zimmer suggested that Mary tie up with a good trade publisher—Kurt Wolff and Pantheon Books. Mary met with Wolff at his office and the Mellons subsequently entered into an agreement with him.[44] In March, Mary sent Jung a telegram informing him that Zimmer had died and she again signed it "love."[45] A long six-page typed letter later followed. It had become possible for letters to be carried across the Atlantic in the diplomatic pouch of a Swiss courier, Adolph Haettenschwiller. Mary began her resumption of correspondence by noting that it had been a long time since they could communicate. Were it not for the Swiss courier, she said, she could not send this letter, which was important to her to get to him. Since his letter of April, 1942, the Bollingen idea had been revived and gone far. The formal letter of July 3, 1942, explained the need to dissolve the Bollingen Foundation; then communications with Switzerland were closed and she was unable to write. She said that the idea of her Press had lain fallow for many months, but then had its own curious revival without great effort by anyone. Things seemed to happen in the right way. Paul and she started the Bollingen Series through another Foundation, the Old Dominion. Kurt Wolff agreed to publish the Series. He had started publishing in the United States about two years previously; the firm's name was Pantheon Books. He had published some high-quality books, including Jacob Burckhardt's *Force and Freedom: Reflections on History*, Paul Claudel's *Coronal*, and Charles Peguy's *Basic Verities*. He seemed to be of like mind with her regarding the merit of works that Jung and she had always had in mind. She decided the Series should be affiliated with Wolff. The Old Dominion Foundation had signed a contract with him to publish Bollingen Series books for a period of two years. Heinrich Zimmer had introduced her to Wolff. He felt Wolff would benefit them greatly because of his long experience in publishing in Europe—the Kurt Wolff Verlag in Munich. Bollingen Series books would be chosen solely by Mary and her associates. Wolff was most enthusiastic about publishing the Series. Said Mary, Stanley Young would be managing editor of the Series. An excellent young man, he had a great deal of experience as an editor with Harcourt Brace. He believed in the purpose of the Series, and had a thorough knowledge of publishing techniques. The Foundation would pay his salary and already had a contract with him. Mary would be the Series' overseer—with no salary nor contract, she jested. The initial announcement of the Series would go out in two months, and the publication date of their first book was October 10. They had a list of six works under consideration. Their first book would be Maud Oakes' *Where the Two Came to Their Father*, an ancient legend of the Navajo, now recorded for the first time from the story given by Jeff King, the Navajo Medicine Man who had become a long-standing friend of Jung since the latter's visit to New Mexico in 1925. Oakes rendered the story into English, and it would be accompanied by eighteen pollen paintings and an introduction by Joseph Campbell, the mythologist. Their second book would be Denis de Rougemont's *La Part du Diable*, scheduled to be published in spring, 1944. De Rougemont was a Swiss writer living in America. His present book, which Mary regarded as provocative and profound, criticized their times, behavior, and the world state of mind while attempting to show by what means a false spirit deformed truths, words, and facts to gain influence over the mind. The other four works on the list were: "The Pyramid Texts of Ancient Egypt," translated by the late James H. Breasted; a volume of essays by Heinrich Zimmer; the *I Ching*, with a preface by Jung; and Jung's *Two Essays on Analytical Psychology*. Their contract with Wolff and their budget limited them to six books per year for the first two years.[46]

Mary then asked Jung to do two things for her, and the second was the main question of her letter. First, she informed him that Cary Baynes had virtually finished the *I Ching*. It could not be published until they had Jung's preface. He now could get the preface to them through Haettenschwiller. Mary was most grateful that Jung had asked him to get in touch with her; she had immediately gone to Washington to see him. She hoped Jung would now write the preface and send it through Haettenschwiller. Then she came to the main question of the letter. She asked for the English-speaking rights to his works. She wanted a statement from him giving the Bollingen Series the English-speaking rights to publish his works that were already in German, those already in English and out of print, and those which he was writing or would write. As she had told him in Zurich years before, her great wish was to get all his works well translated into English and made available to the public. It was impossible to get his works in America, except for the recent ones which would soon be out of print. Young and a lawyer were already working to procure the rights to books already published in America, so that the Bollingen Series could reprint them. As royalties to Jung for the English-speaking rights, she suggested ten percent for the first 2500 copies, twelve and a half percent for the next 2500, and fifteen percent thereafter.[47]

Mary next took up the individual items in Jung's letter of April 10, 1942—that is, the six points contained in her letter previous to that date and in his detailed reply which she was unable to answer at the time.

(1) She understood that he was at work on two volumes of papers and that he had asked her to wait until they were all in order.

(2) "Zosimos" was taken care of in Point (1).

(3) She wondered whether his *Two Essays on Analytical Psychology* had come out in a new edition in German. If so and since he had suggested starting with the *Two Essays*, perhaps he could send it through Haettenschwiller. She would so like to have it on their list for the first year. The *Psychology of the Unconscious*, as he had further suggested, should come next. Translation rights could be ironed out in America. In her opinion, it was one of the most important to make available to the public. It was terribly needed and, even in its present bad translation, impossible to get.

(4) She was perfectly willing to publish Bash's translation of Jung's "Göttliche Kind." She hoped to heaven it had not already gone to Routledge Publishers.

(5) She understood he wished her to wait regarding the "Seven Sermons." She would love to publish it whenever he got around to it, for it was one of her favorite things.

(6) Concerning the first volume of papers, in Point (1), she believed they could procure complete rights from

Farrar and Rinehart Publishing Co. Regarding the translations of papers in the second volume, Mary would make sure that he saw every translation that was done in America before it was printed. And she entirely agreed to publish a third volume of papers—and to publish none of those papers on archetypes separately as monographs. In conclusion, she envisioned the Bollingen Series publishing the following over a period of time: (1) *Two Essays*; (2) *Psychology of the Unconscious*; (3) Vol. I of Papers; (4) Vol. II of Papers; (5) Vol. III of Papers; (6) *Göttliche Kind* and Prof. Karl Kerényi's *Göttliche Mädchen*. It would be a good beginning. From then on they could work out bit by bit the publication of all Jung's works in English. She hoped this exceedingly long letter was clear. They would also arrange for his works to appear in England at the same time, or only slightly later than in America, and they would publish no work of his in English without his approval of publication and translation.[48]

Jung did not respond for six months and he did not give Mary the English-speaking rights to his works.[49] On the occasion of Jung's birthday in July, Mary as usual sent him a telegram wishing him many happy returns and signing it "Love."[50] And Jung, after Christmas and New Year's, sent Mary a brief communication saying that he was happy to have her holiday greetings and that he was well. It was signed: Best wishes, Carl Jung.[51]

Except for brief telegrams there appears to have been little communication between Jung and Mary in 1944. During that year Jung fell ill, and almost died from embolisms in the heart and lungs. Mary cabled to tell him that she had heard he was ill and to inquire whether he was all right. She asked him to cable and she signed the telegram: All love.[52] Jung thanked her and let her know that he was recovering from a serious illness. He was just returned from the hospital, and he was much better. He sent his best wishes.[53] Mary responded that she was so glad that he was better and sent her best wishes for his complete recovery. She said that she missed him terribly and she signed the telegram: All love.[54] A birthday telegram followed on July 26: She hoped that he was improving steadily, wished him happy birthday, and, as usual, signed it: All love.[55]

I found a very interesting page of a typescript of a letter from Eleanor Bertine to Jung, December 10, 1944, among the manuscripts of the Mellon-Jung correspondence at the Jung Archives in Zurich. Dr. Bertine was a leading Jungian analyst in New York City; like Mary, she was a member of the Analytical Psychology Club in New York. In her letter she told Jung that various rumors had come to them for some time, accusing Jung of being pro-Nazi in an apparent effort to discredit his work. An agent of the Federal Bureau of Investigation had interviewed Bertine some weeks previously in an attempt to discover whether Jung was connected with the Nazis and whether he was anti-Semitic. Fortunately, she had several letters from him that cleared up the first point to the agent's apparent satisfaction. On the second point she believed he apparently took her word, for though she gave him Eugene Henley's name as someone who could give rather conclusive evidence on that point, Henley was not interviewed. Bertine asked the agent what possible concern the FBI might have with a Swiss citizen's opinion; the agent replied that he was not allowed to tell her but the FBI had received suspicious information—including the statement that Jung was presently in the United States! Bertine also reported a second recent incident to Jung. There had been a suggestion that she be asked to give a few lectures at a school of adult education in New York, but the idea was met with the undocumented allegation that Jung was pro-Nazi. Bertine told the woman who had suggested the lectures that the woman could tell the school people that Bertine had proof of Jung's point of view if they were really interested. It had to date not been asked for. She cited a third recent incident: A quite liberal weekly [the *New Republic*] had published a review of Brill's *Freud's Contribution to Psychiatry* in which the reviewer irrelevantly stated that Jung had betrayed Freud's progressive viewpoint and that Jung had become one of the most important influences on fascist philosophy in Europe. At present, Bertine went on, it looked to her like a deliberate smear campaign. She suspected that the whole nasty business of charging Jung with being pro-Nazi and anti-Semitic dated from some misrepresentations from the time when he was president of the International Medical Society for Psychotherapy.[56]

Under a Freedom of Information Act request, I examined copies of the FBI reports on Jung. The FBI excised information exempt from disclosure. An FBI Special Agent's report, made at New York City on September 13, 1944, stated that the case originated at New York City as a security matter. At the outset, the agent offered a synopsis of the facts. The details in the report, however, contained much false hearsay. The investigation was launched upon a telephone call from someone—name excised—who advised that he or she had information about an internationally known figure—

Jung—who was definitely pro-Nazi and now said to be in the United States!

From the report, the FBI excised the names and any information that might identify sources. Thus, it is sometimes uncertain whether the same or another person is providing information. In what follows, therefore, I shall refer to each as "a source." Several times during the six to eight months prior to this 1944 report, "a source" had heard that Jung had "turned Nazi," that after Hitler rose to power he had been called from Zurich to Berlin, and that he had become head of a college there and head of medical societies. He or she recently heard that Jung was now in the United States. "A source"—whether the same or another—recently met a man on the bus line from New Rochelle to Larchmont, New York, but did not remember his name. This man stated that Jung was now definitely pro-Nazi and that he might have further information on Jung and his activities. "A source" knew of Jung: He had heard that after Hitler rose to power after 1936 (sic), Jung was called from Switzerland to Berlin and became president of the medical societies after Sigmund Freud had been removed! The source said this would not have occurred unless Jung were 100% Nazi, but he had heard no information that Jung was now in the United States. "A source" furnished a description of Jung. Under the heading, Undeveloped Leads, the agent noted that some persons in New York City who knew Jung would be interviewed concerning whether Jung was presently in the United States and whether his activities were anti-American or pro-Nazi.

A second FBI report was made at New York City on October 28, 1944. An interviewee stated that he learned from a source he could not remember that Jung in his writings seemed an ardent admirer of Hitler. According to this source, Jung had divorced himself from Freud's teachings, and had become a believer in intuition. For Jung, he said, Hitler exemplified intuition. The interviewee reiterated that he could not say whether Jung was engaged in the organization of the German Reich or had assisted the Nazis in any way. On the basis of Jung's philosophy, he considered Jung—with his admiration for Hitler—undoubtedly the philosophical head of the National Socialist movement in Switzerland! A second interviewee—a woman—stated that allegations that Jung was pro-German, an ardent admirer of Hitler, or anti-Semitic were utterly ridiculous. Apparently the same interviewee—perhaps Eleanor Bertine given her letter of December 10, 1944, to Jung—further pointed out that Jung had broken from and attacked theories of Freud and thereby created enmity from some Freudians. Said this interviewee, Jung had psychoanalyzed characters in history, pointing out their good and bad points. Possibly, since he had used Hitler as an instance of some of his theories, some of Freud's followers—interpreting his findings in a political sense—may have branded him pro-German and anti-Semitic. Another interviewee also emphatically denied that Jung was pro-Nazi or anti-Semitic. All interviewed stated that Jung was still in Switzerland. In view of the fact that he was not within the United States, the case was closed.

These FBI reports in 1944 notwithstanding, Jung's letters to Mary Mellon since 1939 clearly show that he was anti-Nazi during World War II—as we have seen.

In the spring of 1945, Haettenschwiller—the Swiss diplomatic courier—carried a message from Jung to Mary. After his careful consideration of the matter, and mindful of experiences in past years, Jung was unable to give her the publishing rights to all his works. He was extremely sorry to disappoint her, but he felt it would be irresponsible to conclude such a far-reaching agreement, given present uncertain conditions. Jung said that he could adapt to current circumstances only if he remained free to publish his works wherever difficulties could most easily be overcome. He had decided to publish his "Psychologie und Alchemie" with Routledge in Britain and in the United States as well. He would not object should Mrs. Mellon want to publish one or another of his works, but he had to reserve his ultimate decision for each individual case. Jung remarked that correspondence was still impossible at present and he did not see what practical steps she could undertake. Pending resumption of postal connections, it seemed to him more sensible for Mrs. Mellon to continue publishing other authors in the Bollingen Series. He realized that Mrs. Mellon would likely be disappointed. His experiences during the past few years made him realize that he would have to await better times and not force matters. He hoped that Mrs. Mellon would appreciate his views.[57]

Mary Mellon was not one to take no easily. Almost immediately, she cabled Jung that she had founded a library of alchemy within the Bollingen Series before she had received his message. She badly wanted his "Psychology and Alchemy." She asked for rights to this one work if at all possible, and she would gladly wait for his decision on other works. The Bollingen Series was off to a very fine beginning with an excellent list. She hoped he was well, asked him to reply, and as usual signed her telegram: All love, Mary Mellon.[58] Jung replied on April 10 that he was sorry, but he had settled with Routledge when American communications were impossible and war issues uncertain. He sent his greetings.[59]

World War II ended in September. Mary was pleased to receive a long letter of four pages from Jung in response to a letter of hers.[60] He told her that her very kind letter should have been answered a while ago, but the backwash of his memorable seventieth birthday and two lectures he gave at Eranos on the "Psychology of the Spirit" kept him busy. He went on to say that it would be nice to see her again after many years of separation and, on his side of the Atlantic, imprisonment. The Swiss, he said, had lived in suspense and a sort of unreality—never too sure of their existence. Several times they might have been invaded. They hardly dared to believe in a miracle, but it came off. His son was an officer in an infantry regiment.

> The war proved to be a great trial to me. People in the army were much better off. They could do something. I only could seek a refuge for my daughter-in-law, who was in the 8th month, and for my grandchildren in the western part of the Alps. That was in the blackest days of May 1940, when France broke down. On account of my critique of the German tyranny I was on the black list of the Gestapo, and if the Germans had invaded Switzerland, I would certainly have been put on the spot. Well informed Germans told me so. My pupils in Germany were forced to repudiate my views publicly. I tell you these things, because you probably have heard the absurd rumor that I am a Nazi. This rumor has been started by the Freudian Jews in America. Their hatred of myself went as far as India, where I found falsified photo's [sic] of mine in the Psychological Seminar of Calcutta University. It was a photo retouched in such a way as to make me appear as an ugly Jew with a pince-nez! These photos came from Vienna! This rumor has been spread over the whole world. Even with us it has been picked up with such alacrity, that I am

forced to publish all the things I have written about Germany. It is however difficult to mention the anti-christianism of the Jews after the horrible things that have happened in Germany. But Jews are not so damned innocent after all—the rôle played by the intellectual Jews in prewar Germany would be an interesting object of investigation. I have challenged the Nazis already in 1934 at a great reception in Frankfort in the house of Baron von Schnitzler, the Director of the I. G. Farben concern. I told them, that their anticlockwise Swastika is whirling down into the abyss of unconsciousness and evil. And this prediction has come off "and how"! After all this you can imagine our inexpressible joy, when we heard, that the Americans had gone ashore in Morocco![61]

Thus Jung denied that he was ever a Nazi, but his letter leaves open the charge of anti-Semitism.

Turning to other subjects, Jung said he had done much work during the War but then a great change occurred in February of 1944. After he slipped on an icy road, broke his fibula, and spent six days in a hospital bed, he had a very bad embolism in the heart and, within about a week, two more embolisms in the lungs. He almost died. He became partially unconscious, partially delirious, and partially ecstatic. Once, during the worst period, he said, he was actually out of his body and he saw the earth from a distance of about 50,000 km: a marvelous sight with India and Ceylon right under his feet and the glorious oceans an indescribable luminous blue.[62] He saw other great things that by no means meant delirium. Then he got a thrombosis of both legs up to the abdomen. He had spent four and a half months in the hospital and was a complete wreck when he returned home. Since then, Jung reported, he had picked up again, though slowly. Because his heart had a scar he had to walk slowly and avoid exertions of all sorts, including mental effort. The amount of work he could do was limited but he said he could work quietly with his books and he wrote a number of things in the past year. He could go sailing and he could even do a bit of rowing. He could walk for one hour or more. He had grown thinner but that was mainly due to their forced vegetarian diet and lack of fat. He could smoke and they still had decent tobacco. If she could send something like English tobacco or "Granger" from the United States, however, it would be most welcome. He was afraid he had become a greedy old European, he joked! Jung went on to say that thirty-five years ago he had told the late Medill McCormick that the United States was on the march to domination of the Pacific and to the *Imperium Americanum*. McCormick laughed, but President Harry Truman cannot laugh with a skeleton in the cupboard—the atomic bomb. Jung thought that Europe was dying. The center of gravity had shifted to America—and to the atomic bomb. Jung said his old brain tried to cope with the most unbelievable catastrophes that the world had ever witnessed. They were all shaken from top to bottom. Mary's husband was not the only one. In conclusion, Jung said that traveling would be impossible or a hardship for a long time. Consequently, he restrained his hopes of seeing her soon again. If she did come over she would find a different Europe. Switzerland, however, was still a paradise of peace where little had changed. He was a prisoner in paradise and he had nothing of which to complain. His present letter was extravagantly long, but it was very nice to chat with her again—*un plaisir inespéré*. He signed the letter: Yours affectionately, C. G. Jung.[63]

In 1945, Jung submitted "The Psychology of the

Transference" (in German) for publication. He may have had Mary among others in mind when he wrote:

> The patient, by bringing an activated unconscious content to bear upon the doctor, constellates the corresponding unconscious material in him . . . contents are often activated in the doctor which might normally remain latent. . . .
> Even the most experienced psychotherapist will discover again and again that he is caught up in a bond, a combination resting on mutual unconsciousness. And though he may believe himself to be in possession of all the necessary knowledge concerning the constellated archetypes, he will in the end come to realize that there are very many things indeed of which his academic knowledge never dreamed.[64]

To his letter of September 24, Mary replied by telegram: Bless him, it arrived as always at exactly the right moment. She was glad he was better, and she was sending tobacco. She signed: All love.[65] Four days later she telegraphed again that she would get a book on Paracelsus if it was important to him and he wanted it.[66] Jung responded the same day: Yes, with pleasure.[67]

Mary then wrote an eight-page letter.[68] She began:

> You will never know what joy your long letter gave me. It was so long and complete and told me exactly what I wanted to know. I had to cable you when I received it. As I told you in the cable, it arrived at exactly the moment I needed it most. By some miracle they have always done just that.
> In the meantime I received your cable in answer to mine about the Paracelsus book. You remember that I wanted to give you the "Splendor Solis" before I left Zurich, and that it had been sold. This then is my 70th birthday present to you. From all I could find out about it, it is a very rare book, containing 10 parts to the British Museum's 4. But I didn't want to go ahead with it until I was sure you wanted it. You may have it in your hands by this time. It comes to you with my

great love. If it is as rare as they say, no rarer person could receive it.

It appears that I may be able to publish your "Psychology and Alchemy" after all. I have gone to all lengths in England (personal emissaries, cables, letters—all but myself) to find out the exact status of the book in relation to American rights. Routledge says no one has the option and I am negotiating for it now.

You see—within the Bollingen Series I want to found a Library of Alchemy. I have already published Plato's "Timaeus"—and yours as the next would be perfect. There is no such thing in the whole world, I am sure, as a Library of Alchemy.

Mary had intended to come to Zurich in summer 1946. She rightly and eloquently told Jung that she was convinced that she had begun something of value in the Bollingen Series:

I am very excited over the way our idea has worked out in the world. I am convinced that I have started something of value. As in all beginnings, this has had many stumbling blocks and I have made mistakes. But the underlying principle is right—that I know.[69]

The personal had always been intermixed with the Bollingen idea to Mary. She went on to tell him:

But I must see you—myself—you and I had the idea together and I cannot rest until I am with you again. I must talk to you, Dr. Jung, about so many things—I am tied up in this idea, my personal life is, I mean, I have conflicts which only you will understand, and you must help me too in the long range plan about yourself.

I can only tell you this. In face of the criticism which you relayed to me and which I have heard here, and in consideration of the people you have behind you in this country and England, I am absolutely certain that I can be of great service to you with the outlet I have started. It needs authority behind it which I have acquired (God knows why except for my great love for you which all must feel is more than a passing fancy) and it needs the funds which I have at my disposal. It needs wisdom which I am gaining as time goes on, and it needs a certain moving in a sure direction without looking to right or left, sure in the direction and the goal to which it points—and no hysteria about you and your work.

With your help I want to gather you up, so to speak, for the future. That is the backbone of the Bollingen Series—and what I am working toward. At the same time I mean to publish works that are pertinent and of fine quality to go alongside of you. It is much like Eranos, in print. Your fertilization of all those lectures has made Eranos. Yet you needed and will always need the other ones around you to feed you and bring in the ideas which need fertilization. To no one except those working with me have I expressed this.[70]

She continued:

But I must talk to you. I need you myself on top of all this, as you must know. Whatever brought us together I don't know—but I do know it was meant to be, and that I am meant to do something about us.

You must look like the bust Toni Wolff has of you, when you were much younger, if you are thin. Take care and stay as well as you can during this hard winter to come. The famine in Europe is too frightful to think about. I am sending you 11 pounds a week, made up of butter (or fats) and sugar. Let me know what else you want in the packages. Coffee? Tea? If what we send carries properly then I will send more to you and others.

Let me hear from you again as soon as you can.

In conclusion: "I hope Mrs. Jung is well and all your family. Please give her my kindest regards and my love to Toni." She signed the letter: All my love to you, Mary. A postscript said: "I can feel all through me how I will feel when I lay eyes on you again." All in all, it was a remarkable letter. It is prescient regarding the

Bollingen Series, and it expresses the strength of her feelings of connection to Jung.[71]

Jung may have felt that Mary was again becoming too much identified with him, and the tone of his reply was somewhat more distant than his previous letter. He thanked her for her messages and her letter. His answer was delayed since he was swamped by correspondence since his birthday. Her Bollingen plan needed further discussion that could not be done by letter. They would have to wait until she arrived in Switzerland. She may have heard—Jung announced—that Routledge & Kegan Paul in London was planning to publish his whole work. He and she would have to talk about "Psychology and Alchemy" since he had signed a contract with Routledge & Kegan Paul that included American rights. A special alchemy series within the Bollingen Series would not be worthwhile—nobody save for very few scholars could grasp "that abstruse stuff." Even his own book on alchemy needed a background of psychological commentary and other comparative studies to be acceptable. She was very kind to send some foodstuffs, but they in Switzerland could not acquire items that were rationed without giving up the same amount of rationing cards. Their state of nutrition was completely satisfactory. Things had become much better in Switzerland since 1944. Only his supply of English tobacco might fade away. He was practically as busy as ever, but he had to go a little slower since he needed his relaxation. His daily prayer was to emerge from the ocean of letters. For Switzerland to be surrounded by the Nazis had been horrible, but it had one advantage for him—it considerably lessened his correspondence. He had heard that Paul Mellon was with General Dwight Eisenhower's staff, and he had hoped that Paul would turn up in Zurich with other American officers, but he had not. Jung hoped that he was all right and that he had an interesting time during the War. Jung said he was looking forward with pleasure to Mary's visit. Traveling now seemed simple by airplane. He expressed all good wishes and many thanks, and he concluded the letter: I remain yours cordially, C. G. Jung.[72] Mary's Christmas and New Year's greetings by telegram expressed her hope that he was well, awaited his letter, said she would send no more food, and sent all love for Christmas and the New Year.[73]

In January, 1946, Mary cabled that the Bollingen Series had asked Rascher Verlag for exclusive English language rights to *Psychologische Betrachtungen*, edited by Jolande Jacobi, in 1945. She was happy to tell Jung that Routledge had given the Bollingen Series first option to American rights for *Psychologie und Alchemie*. She signed the telegram: Love.[74] On January 15, Jung's secretary informed Mary that Jung still had not received the Paracelsus volumes because the Swiss bookseller could not accept payment in blocked dollars. Mary, however, might find a way of paying in Swiss francs. Jung was sorry that the gift should cause her so much trouble and he was willing to wait until financial transactions became less complicated.[75] On January 16, Jung cabled to let Mary know that he was all right and slowly recovering from a spell of illness.[76]

Now that travel was again possible across the Atlantic to Switzerland, Mary wanted to do some analytical work with Jung. In April, she informed him that she could come to Switzerland in July, and she asked if she could work with him. She said that she needed to see him badly. She would then go on to Ascona and return to America after the Eranos Conference. If he was in

Bollingen she would try to arrange to stay nearby if possible. She hoped he was well, asked him to please reply, and sent all love.[77]

Jung wrote Mary a detailed reply. He thanked her for several books of the Bollingen Series and for others that she had sent. He found the book by Paul Radin (*The Road of Life and Death*, on a ritual drama of the Winnebago) especially interesting. Her plan to come over in July collided with his badly needed vacations. He added that he could arrange, however, to see her for about a fortnight in August at Bollingen, where he would be before the Eranos meeting began on August 29. He would advise her to stay in Zurich since no hotel near Bollingen would suit her. There was a nicely located, somewhat old-fashioned place in Rapperswil (an attractive old town on the Lake of Zurich between Zurich and Bollingen), but it perhaps was a bit too simple for her taste. In Zurich, she could rent a car and drive out to Bollingen—a distance of about 35 km. Since his illness, he reiterated, he needed more rest and needed to economize his strength. He always thought she might come in May—a better time—but if they did the analytical work in a compressed way they could do much in a fortnight.

Jung remarked that Switzerland was still full of troubles; peacetime differed not very greatly from wartime. Their food problem had improved, though bread rations still were low. They had 250 grams of bread—in Germany, people had but 200. The Swiss, however, had the advantage of other foodstuffs that were impossible to obtain in other countries. Their conditions were decidedly better than those in Britain. Apart from these food conditions, she would find Switzerland what it used to be eight years ago. Even automobiles were running again. He hoped that she was always in good health, and sent his best regards to Paul Mellon. He closed: I remain, yours cordially.[78]

Mary was very pleased to get Jung's letter telling her that he would see her in August. She booked a flight to Geneva on July 30 and expected to be settled in Zurich by about August 2. She made a reservation at the Baur au Lac in Zurich; though she thought the little hotel in Rapperswil might be more pleasant, it would probably be more convenient to be in Zurich. She informed Jung that she was becoming excited about her trip and had so much about which to talk to him in every direction. The Paracelsus book had not yet arrived, but he should have it for his birthday rather than for Christmas. Since her last letter, Jack Barrett, her Associate Editor, had met—and had a very satisfactory discussion with—Herbert Read of Kegan Paul. Mary was having a long discussion with Kegan Paul that week, too. She had great hope of a wonderful collaboration between Kegan Paul and the Bollingen Series regarding his works. She informed Jung that Barrett would come to Europe in the latter part of August and to the Eranos meeting. Mary wanted personally to introduce Jung to him. He was an excellent editor, and their list of books was becoming more and more interesting. Zimmer's *Myth and Symbol in Hindu Art* would appear within a week, and she would send a copy to Jung and Toni Wolff immediately. She was sure he would be delighted with it. She was looking forward to seeing him with such pleasure as she could not express, and she thanked him for his letters. She signed the letter: Affectionately yours, Mary Mellon.[79]

A letter on Bollingen Series stationery followed: Mary informed Jung that many interesting things had re-

sulted from her long talk with Herbert Read of Kegan
Paul. He, Barrett, and Mary herself had gone over a plan
of the publication of his entire works. Read had for
some years the same feeling as she—that a uniform edition of his works was highly necessary for both Britain
and America. The difficulty for his firm had been the
question of financing the project. Read agreed with her
that the edition should be as perfect as possible in for-
mat, typography, translation, and editorial supervision.
The Bollingen Foundation could offer the necessary financial assistance. Read explained that only with this
sort of assistance could Kegan Paul undertake a defini-
tive edition of Jung's works. They planned to set up an
editorial board consisting of an editor-in-chief, an editor
for translations, a representative of Jung in Zurich,
Read from Kegan Paul, and Mary as the representative
of Bollingen. The Foundation would bear the major part
of the expenses of the editorial board. They had agreed
on the above plans, and Mary was writing to Jung about
the selection of an editor-in-chief. Read told them that
when he spoke with Jung in Zurich, Jung was in favor
of Michael Fordham, an Englishman. Mary frankly
knew no one in the United States who could fill the position. If it met with Jung's approval they would decide
on Fordham. Read, Barrett, Mary, Jung, and perhaps
Fordham could meet in Ascona to discuss the plan thoroughly and to decide on an editor for translations and
on Jung's representative. Of the persons associated with
Jung, Toni Wolff stood out in Mary's mind as the one
who understood his work best. Jolande Jacobi had also
been mentioned for the position. Mary knew that she
had done good work on Jung's works. She remembered
meeting Jacobi in Ascona and, frankly, she did not like
her very much, but that might have been a first impres-

sion only. In Jung's view she might be better suited to be his representative, or he might have another suggestion. Still, Mary said, she was hoping he would suggest Toni Wolff. The first step, however, was a decision on the editor-in-chief. She asked for Jung's view on Fordham or his suggestion of anyone else whom he might prefer. Paul Mellon and she were extremely pleased to have found in Kegan Paul the perfect collaboration with Britain—and in Herbert Read a man who had the edition of Jung's works at heart as much as they had. She was very glad that the Bollingen Series would play its part in getting his books into a worthy edition. She hoped he approved.[80]

Jung replied that he could not answer fully, but he wanted to let her know his thoughts about the question of the editor-in-chief. He told her that he was not well enough acquainted with Fordham to be sure that he would be the right man. Read and himself, said Jung, had not known who else in Britain to consider. Jung wanted to make no decision of any sort before he came to a definite agreement with Kegan Paul. He had not heard from Read since he was in Switzerland last December. He suggested they postpone a decision until the summer. Her idea of a meeting in Ascona of Read, Barrett, Fordham, her, and him was splendid. They could discuss the question of the editor-in-chief at that time. He apologized for the shortness of the letter, but said he was in the midst of a flood of work.[81]

Mary thought Jung right in wanting to come to an agreement with Kegan Paul before they made any definite arrangement, she replied. She thought that Read, Barrett, Jung, and herself should perhaps have a preliminary meeting before they see a prospective editor-in-chief. Another prospect had occurred to Paul and herself: Violet de Laszlo, a very intelligent woman thoroughly conversant with all of Jung's work. But they could discuss the prospect of Fordham or de Laszlo in Ascona. Mary added that the Paracelsus volumes were finally in her hands and they would be shipped to him from New York this week. She asked for his approval or disapproval of her points contained in this letter about an editor-in-chief; she would communicate his reply to Read. After that, she believed all of their preliminary arrangements would be made and she would wait to see him in Switzerland.[82]

Jung did not yet know what arrangements Mary had made with Read. He had only told Jung that he would like Fordham as editor-in-chief. Fordham, however, had written to Jung that he would agree to have Gerhard Adler's help for the German part of the translations. Although Jung had full confidence in de Laszlo, he did not see how she could come in on the project since there were already two people concerned with the translations. There were, said Jung, complicated questions that could hardly be dealt with by letter. He would like to postpone discussion of the whole situation until their meeting in Ascona. He proposed that Mary and Paul Mellon, Barrett, Read, and himself be present at the meeting. He would bring his secretary, Marie-Jeanne Schmid, to take notes. He also proposed waiting until the main questions were settled before appointing editors. Though he knew very little of Fordham, Jung commented that he had felt much better since Fordham was willing to accept Adler's help. Fordham told Jung that Read was agreeable to Adler's cooperation. Jung expressed his special gratitude for the interest Mary Mellon took in the publication of his works. He had revised the *Psychology of the Unconscious* in German and it had become practically a new book.[83]

Barrett and Mary sent Read a formal letter: It reported that, after conferring with Mr. and Mrs. Mellon and the officers of the Bollingen Foundation in Washington, the Foundation agreed in principle on all the points in the proposed collaboration with Kegan Paul for the joint publication of Jung's complete works in English. The Foundation's decision was based on the preliminary talk outlining the plan which Read, Mary Mellon, and Barrett had in New York in May. The Foundation's officers requested that Kegan Paul draw up a statement embodying the terms of an agreement under which they would enter into this joint endeavor. They suggested that the statement contain, besides points already agreed to and related details, any others occurring to Kegan Paul. This statement, and the reply of the Foundation's officers, would provide a basis for their talks with Jung and might help them in arriving at the final agreement. They believed that it would serve to state their joint intention, outline necessary questions about the joint publication, and signify to Jung that, with his approval, they were prepared to reach a final agreement. Barrett was sending a copy of this letter to Jung, and he asked that Jung be sent a copy of Read's reply.[84] On June 24, Mary herself wrote Jung a brief letter on Bollingen Series stationery and enclosed this formal letter to Read that she and Barrett had composed the past weekend when Barrett had been at Oak Spring, her home. She believed it clearly set forth the situation at the moment, and she hoped Jung approved.[85]

In mid-July, Mary suddenly canceled her plans to go to Zurich. This was in part because she had not yet recovered from a recent operation, but there was another reason as well. She had consulted the *I Ching* on whether to make the trip to Europe; she had got exhaustion as the "prognosis." She had been and was exhausted. She concluded that it was not the time to go.[86]

Jung was surprised to receive a telegram on July 17 in which Mary announced that she was not coming to Switzerland. The telegram stated that owing to a recent operation doctors felt it was inadvisable for her to make the trip. Barrett was taking her reservation. Otherwise the plan was the same as before, except Mary felt that it might be well to meet with Read in Zurich before Ascona. She said that a letter would follow explaining fully. She could not tell him how disappointed she was. She signed the telegram: Love, Mary Mellon.[87]

On the same day, Mary wrote Jung a letter two and a quarter pages of typescript in length on Bollingen Series stationery. She explained that about six weeks previously she had undergone a rather severe operation, but felt that she would be recovered in time to make the trip. When she had been examined recently, however, all felt it was very unwise for her to undertake any trip that summer. She could not begin to tell him how upset and disappointed she was, for she was anxious to see him and to participate in the meeting with Read and Barrett. Barrett was taking her reservation on July 31 and, after going to Paris and perhaps London, he would arrive in Zurich about August 15. He was a Trustee of the Bollingen Foundation and he understood the problems involved in the joint venture with Kegan Paul. He and Mary felt that the meeting between Jung, Barrett, and Read would be better held before the Eranos Conference at Ascona began, for she knew how busy Jung would be there. Since Jung had set aside some time for her at Bollingen, Mary expressed hope

that he could see Barrett at least two or three times before Read arrived. If Read could not meet Barrett and
Jung in Zurich before the Eranos Conference, they
could meet him afterwards in Ascona. Barrett and she
had gone over the Kegan Paul situation very thoroughly. Mary then went on to introduce Barrett, saying
that she had known him for fifteen years, and he had
become one of Paul's and her best friends. He was not
in the Bollingen Series at its beginning, but toward the
end of its second year he did some work on its mailing
lists. When her former editor resigned to pursue his
own affairs, Barrett became Associate Editor. He had
absorbed a great deal of the meaning of the Series, he
had the idea behind it at heart, and he was dedicated to
helping her develop that idea. He had as good judgment
as any man that Paul, the Foundation, and she knew.
He was well able to represent them with Jung and with
Eranos. She was sure he would do a good job.[88]

In his reply, Jung said he was quite shocked by the
news of her operation and he was disappointed that she
could not come to Ascona. He had been looking forward to their interviews with great expectations. He
was grateful for her careful introduction of Barrett; he
would see Barrett several times as she wished. He
would be glad to discuss the situation before the actual
business meeting. The situation appeared to him a bit
complicated, for he was not fully informed about its details, but that could wait until Barrett gave him the
complete information. He hoped she would soon re-
cover from the aftermath of her operation and sent his
very best wishes.[89]

Barrett's meetings with Jung went well, and at the
business meeting in Ascona, Jung, Read, Barrett, and
Fordham reached general agreement on the important

matters. Barrett told Mary that he came away with a feeling of exaltation.[90]

During the 1940s, Mary had recurrent attacks of asthma that placed a strain on her heart. In early October, she and Paul were returning from a hunt when an attack began. Her atomizer containing a medication had broken, and the attack grew more severe. She was put to bed at Oak Spring, but she suffered another attack that was too much for her heart. There she died at the age of forty-two.[91] John Barrett arrived at Oak Spring the following day. Paul Mellon immediately told him that Mary's death would not prevent their going on together to accomplish what she had wanted.[92] Barrett cabled Jung the tragic news that Mary Mellon had died suddenly and all were grieving.[93]

The news of Mary's death moved Jung; he wrote Paul Mellon that it caused such a shock to him that he could realize how terrible it must have been to Paul. Jung wrote that she was a woman who had it in her to play a great role in the world. He shared Paul's grief and suffering.[94]

In November, Paul Mellon cabled to thank Jung for his kind expression of sympathy. He emphasized that the Bollingen Foundation and Series would continue under Barrett and him in accordance with the same principles and policies to which Mary was dedicated—including the re-publication of Jung's works. He sent his kindest personal regards to Jung and Mrs. Jung.[95]

When the contracts for *The Collected Works* were signed in August of 1947, Jung stipulated that the first volume be published within three years, save for war, governmental restrictions, or acts of God. Three times he reluctantly granted a year's extension, until 1953 when the first volume appeared. Mary Mellon had hoped to make Jung's works available as soon as possible. Everyone now involved, including the veteran publishers at Pantheon and at Routledge & Kegan Paul, had expected at the outset that the volumes would appear more quickly than they did. No one involved had realistically regarded the problems of the logistics of editorial operations strung out between London, New York, and Switzerland. Even Jung contributed to the deliberate pace by continuing to revise old works and to turn out new ones that had to be translated. Eventually *The Collected Works* appeared, and in the end totaled eighteen volumes.[96]

Mary Mellon had developed a transatlantic community of support between herself and Jung and for his works. From the U.S. side of the Atlantic, Paul Mellon generously continued the support that led to the publication of Jung's *Collected Works*. Many years after Mary's death, Franz Jung remembered his father speaking to him of his admiration for her and awe for her drive: she got things done.[97]

Part II

C. G. Jung and J. B. Priestley

In 1946—the same year that Mary Mellon died—
Jung's friendship with J. B. Priestley began; that friendship promoted a greater awareness of Jung's psychology
in Britain. Priestley, who had read all Jung's books published in England, proposed to do a British Broadcasting
Corporation radio talk on Jung and his work, and to em-
phasize the importance of his psychology in the social
and political areas. Their mutual friend, Gerhard Adler,
had written to Jung on Priestley's behalf, and Jung had
agreed to see Priestley should the latter come to Zurich
in May. To meet Jung, Priestley decided to visit Switzerland then, and he looked forward to the event.[1] In response, Jung invited Priestley and his wife to a quite in-
formal dinner at the Jungs.[2]

The two men hit it off well. Priestley enjoyed his first
meeting with Jung enormously, and after visiting Beat-
enberg, Berne, and Ascona, he and his family returned
to Zurich. He hoped to have a second meeting.[3] The
Jungs invited Priestley, Mrs. Jane Priestley, and their
two daughters to supper that Sunday.[4]

The script of Priestley's broadcast talk on June 18,

1946, is in the BBC Written Archives, in Reading, Berkshire. Priestley began the talk by noting that he was not a psychologist, and that his talk was addressed to fellow laypersons who often wondered what went on inside their minds, why they sometimes behaved so strangely, and whether they could do anything about it. Priestley also said he had read Jung for years and regarded him not only as an original thinker in our time but also as one of its few liberators. Priestley said further that he had long believed that behind much of this age's bitterness and violence was modern people's sense of homelessness, contempt for oneself, despair. However much of the poet or mystic there might be in Jung, thought Priestley, his methods of research had been scientific, and his evidence was based on years of careful observation, analysis, and clinical work. Jung had decisively broken with Freud and the Viennese psychoanalysts who had dealt primarily with patients suffering from neuroses, victims of repressed memories of early experiences.

Priestley also remarked how Jung saw that the theory on which psychoanalysis was based was far too limited. He had been a psychiatrist at an asylum in Zurich where he had studied the fantasies of the truly demented and insane. The unconscious that produced these fantasies, often showing marked traces of the worldwide symbolism of myth and folklore, was clearly not the unconscious described by Freudians. Jung evolved his theory of the collective unconscious below the level of the personal unconscious and as much part of our psychic inheritance as the digestive and reproductive systems were part of our physical inheritance. It was the vast magical world within us—enslaving the criminal or the insane, inspiring the poet or prophet.

Though it had not yet taken its proper place among our ideas, it enlarged human beings rather than cutting them down and it rooted them to their kind and to the earth, instead of separating them and deepening their sense of loneliness. Priestley suggested that this talk was no place to discuss Jung's theory of the archetypes or the ebb and flow of psychic energy. It was perhaps sufficient to say this unconscious wanted its life, even as the conscious mind did. And it had, Jung insisted, its own wisdom, like the ancient mother it was. It was an essential part of our real selves, which were something quite different from our mere egos. Any one-sidedness in our conscious minds was compensated in the unconscious. Jung, Priestley further remarked, had worked out an ingenious system of opposites: extraversion and introversion, and also the opposed functions of thinking and feeling, sensation and intuition. If we were unaware of this process, we were liable to find ourselves in the grip of forces we did not understand and, by projecting contents of the unconscious onto the outside world, to be deluded. This applied to us not only as individuals but also as members of communities, which enabled Jung to use analytical psychology to understand behavior in nations and history. For instance, he pointed out that there were demonic forces in the unconscious that were now terribly dangerous to modern Western people who, unlike people at any other time, pretended they did not exist. The great religions, primarily by means of symbol and ritual, had kept these forces in check. Modern people tried to ignore the unconscious, and, pretending these demonic forces did not exist, they then found themselves at their mercy. The Germans, a scientifically educated nation, allowed Hitler to bewitch them, and then all the dark forces of the unconscious—demons we had pretended to exorcise from the world—raged unchecked, and the most fantastic cruelties and monstrous perversions were let loose. Jung had warned this might happen, starting nearly thirty years ago, when he pointed out, after closely studying German character, mythology, and literature, that he could hear the pacing of beasts in their subterranean dungeon—threatening an outburst with devastating consequences. There had been, Priestley continued, some silly rumors lately that Jung had shown pro-Nazi sympathies. Priestley would as soon expect a cancer specialist to have pro-cancer sympathies. Jung's warning remained. We were not out of the sinister wood yet. We still ignored our unconscious processes. The dangerous business of projection—i.e., of throwing the more evil contents of one's unconscious onto other people—still went on. Another fruitful and liberating idea of Jung, said Priestley, was his theory of individuation. Most of us who were past our later thirties had felt difficulties, and so forth, that had left us deeply disturbed or depressed. Jung's researches had led him to specialize in psychological problems of the middle-aged, which, as a rule, could not be solved by discovering what happened to them in the nursery. Jung had said that the first half of life—really the field of ordinary psychoanalysis—was essentially a preparation for life—mating, earning a living, adjusting egos to the world—but that the second half, starting in the late thirties, was really a preparation for death. Though at first sight it may appear gloomy or futile, there was a profound wisdom in the idea. From middle-age onwards, so as to live fully and not sink into vain regrets, we need to adopt a different standpoint from that of youth. We have to detach ourselves from the mere biological procession, live more in the spirit, and ally our-selves more with what is imperishable and outside the ego. We must attempt to release ourselves from the tug-of-war of the opposites—conscious and unconscious—to achieve a new synthesis—moving from the ego to the larger self, a long elaborate process. Priestley real-ized the inadequacy of this account of the matter, but his point was that here, in a psychology based soundly on scientific method, we drew nearer to both Christian insights and the ancient wisdom of the East. Perhaps Jung's greatest achievement was this: using the instru-ment of the modern West—the scientific intellect—he had cleared a way through dark jungles into mountain air. Priestley concluded that the man who had used that blade, gone into the darkness and come out again into sunlight—where we might follow—was one of our great liberators.

Priestley's BBC broadcast was enormously successful with Jung.

I have heard from many people who came from England and through letters, how much it was appreciated and how excellently you succeeded in presenting the essence of my ideas. Unfortunately in spite of all efforts I could not hear your broadcast since all British stations were inaudible due to atmospheric disturbances. All the other people here who knew about this broadcast tried also in vain to listen in. No-body in Switzerland has heard it as far as I know. We were very disappointed indeed! Would there be a possibility of hav-ing your manuscript, so that I could get an idea of how you did it?

Since I saw you I have read several of your novels and plays and I enjoyed them very much. I was particularly impressed by the two aspects of your personality. Your one face is so much turned to the world that one is surprised again and again to meet another face which is turned to the great abyss of all things. I just wanted to tell you my impression as I want to let you know how much I appreciate the superhuman faculty of looking at things with a straight and with an inverted eye.[5]

After the broadcast, Priestley received many letters of congratulation from psychologists and others who knew something about analytical psychology, and he also fielded numerous inquiries requesting the titles of Jung's books. He was delighted to send Jung a copy of his BBC broadcast, yet it was designed to be heard rather than read. He was happy to learn that Jung had read several of his novels and plays since his visit. He was sending Jung a copy of his new novel, *Bright Day*, which was one of his best. Meeting Jung, Priestley noted, had been a privilege and a pleasure for him.[6]

Jung was even more impressed by Priestley's broadcast after he had read it; he had never seen a better summary of his main ideas in such a concise form—he called it a masterpiece! In his letter of 9 August 1946, Jung said that he immensely enjoyed Priestley's luminous and comprehensive talk. It was remarkable how Priestley had succeeded in getting the vast subject together and making a whole of it. Jung said he had also read Priestley's latest novel with great interest. He was impressed, first, by the way in which Priestley made his characters real, and secondly, by the atmosphere Priestley gave to places and situations. As a psychologist Jung noticed the extroverted hero who lived the better part of his life forgetting nothing but himself and his relatedness to certain human beings. An introvert would have forgotten the greater part of the world! Gregory, the hero, needed thirty years and a bad slump into a prolonged depression in order to remember himself. An introvert—if the gods were favorable—would need thirty years or more to discover how attractive people could be.[7]

After Priestley's broadcast on Jung, the BBC wanted Jung to give a talk. Jung, however, initially declined. In September, Priestley wrote Jung that the organizers had asked him to add his voice to their appeal. He noted that this particular program was intended for intelligent and educated listeners. As he knew from his own talk on Jung—which had been done only on the general program—there certainly was now in Britain a great interest in Jung and his work. Priestley closed his letter in haste since he was busy with two new plays at the moment.[8]

Priestley's note had its effect: Jung reconsidered his decision and agreed to do a talk for the BBC. He, too, was somewhat overwhelmed by various obligations at the moment, but he had his secretary thank Priestley and let him know that he had decided to do the talk.[9] Indeed, in September, Jung was Winston Churchill's dinner companion at an official reception given by the City of Zurich during Churchill's visit to Switzerland.[10]

Jung gave his broadcast talk in the Third Programme of the British Broadcasting Corporation on November 3, 1946. Entitled "The Fight with the Shadow," it was first published in The Listener (London) on November 7.[11] In the broadcast, Jung gave a psychological perspective on the events of the previous decade: he said that he regarded his opinion as no more than one contribution to the enormously complicated task of finding a comprehensive explanation. Taking up the events in Germany, he commented that the psychopathology of the masses is rooted in the psychology of individuals. One needed successfully to establish that certain symptoms or phenomena were common to a number of different individuals to begin to examine the analogous mass phenomena. As early as 1918, Jung said that he had noticed peculiar disturbances in the unconscious of his German patients. Non-personal phenomena were manifesting themselves in dreams as mythological motifs; he observed that these archetypes expressed primitivity, violence, and cruelty. Though the onslaught of primitive forces was by no means a purely Teutonic phenomenon, as the following years made evident, the German mentality proved to be more susceptible. Jung suggested that the proneness of Germans to mass psychology and the defeat and social disaster consequent to World War I made it more probable that Germany would be victim of a mass movement resulting from an upheaval of forces lying dormant in the unconscious—ready to break through all moral barriers. Jung reiterated his observation that the tide rising in the unconscious after World War I had been reflected in individual dreams as those mythological symbols expressing primitivity, violence, and cruelty. When such symbols occurred in a large number of individuals and were not consciously understood, they started to draw these individuals together and a mob might be formed. Its leader would be found in the individual who had the least resistance and the greatest will to power: that individual would loose everything that was ready to burst forth, and the mob would follow. Jung was aware of the danger involved when such people crowded together, but he did not know at the time whether there were enough of them in Germany to cause an explosion. Following up quite a number of individual cases, however, Jung suggested that he could observe these forces as they broke through the individual's moral and intellectual self-control. If the individual clung to a shred of reason or preserved the bonds of human relationships, however, new symbols appeared in the unconscious, this time reflecting the forces of order. They represented a gleam of hope.[12]

Jung went on to speak of the present day. The worldwide confusion and disorder reflected a similar condition in the mind of the individual. Jung said that if the symbols of order in the unconscious were not integrated into consciousness, then the forces they expressed would accumulate to a dangerous degree—just as the forces of destruction and disorder did after World War I. Only the moral leaders of mankind—not the political leaders—were capable of such an achievement. The value and importance of the individual, however, were rapidly decreasing and the chances of his or her being heard would vanish more and more. Through the unconscious, Jung remarked, man has gambled away his fundamental rights. Germany had provided us with an example of the psychological development in question. Large portions of the population were uprooted by industrialization and herded together in large centers. This new way of existence—with its mass psychology and social dependence on the fluctuation of wages and markets—produced individuals unstable, insecure, and suggestible. The system of moral and political education in Germany, moreover, had in Jung's view done its utmost to permeate people with a spirit of dull obedience, and with the belief that every desirable thing must come from the State. The individual's feeling of weakness was compensated by the eruption of previously unknown desires for power. The avalanche rolled on and produced its leader. What was his original intention? Hitler dreamed of a "new order." Deep down in his being, he was motivated by the forces of order that became operative in him when desirousness and greed had taken complete possession of his conscious mind. Hitler was the exponent of a "new order"—and that, said Jung, is why Germans fell for him. They wanted order, but they made the mistake of choosing the principal victim of disorder for their leader. Even as they were greedy for power, they were greedy for order. Hitler symbolized something in every individual: he represented to an overwhelming degree the shadow, the inferior part of every personality.[13]

What could the German people have done? Jung asked. They should have seen their own shadows, he answered. If, on the contrary, French Swiss, for example, projected their own shadows and assumed that German Swiss were all devils, then might Switzerland have civil war. The only struggle really worthwhile was the fight against the overwhelming power drive of the shadow. The individual was the sole carrier of mind and life. Society and the state derived their quality from the mental condition of individuals: they were made up of individuals and their organizations. Jung said that people ought refrain from using the word "State" as though it referred to a sort of super-individual endowed with inexhaustible power and resourcefulness. The dangerous slope down to mass psychology started with the plausible thinking in big numbers—and in terms of powerful organizations, where the individual dwindled to a mere nothing. Everything that exceeded a certain human size evoked equally inhuman powers in the unconscious. Totalitarian demons were called forth, instead of the realization that all that could really be accomplished was an infinitesimal step forward in the moral nature of the individual.[14]

Priestley and Jung had become such good friends that

in the following year, 1947, Mrs. Jane Priestley wrote to Jung when one of the Priestleys' daughters suffered from a psychological illness.[15] Jung immediately replied.[16] The illness is discussed in Vincent Brome's biography, *J. B. Priestley*.[17]

Both Priestley and Jung were busy men who did not always have time to correspond with each other. In 1947–48, Jung was preparing three new German volumes and working on *Mysterium Coniunctionis*, amid other work that included the founding of the C. G. Jung Institute.[18] Priestley, meanwhile, was continuing his prolific literary career. Between 1946 and 1949, he produced no fewer than six plays—*Ever Since Paradise, The Linden Tree, The Rose and Crown, Home is Tomorrow, The Golden Fleece*, and *Summer's Day Dream*—not to mention essays, journalism, and lectures.[19]

In January, 1948, the British Council in Zurich was threatened with closure; consequently, the Council asked Jung to help. Feeling that the matter was important and rather urgent, Jung asked Priestley—who was a staunch supporter of British-Swiss relations—if the latter could also help by appealing to the powers-that-be in whatever way he considered appropriate.[20] A subsequent letter thanked Priestley for his helpful kindness. Jung was glad as well to hear that the Priestleys' daughter was much better.[21]

In September of 1949, Priestly sent Jung his newest book, *Delight*. Jung was away from his home on Seestrasse in Küsnacht at the time, but his secretary informed Priestley that the gift had arrived.[22] Meanwhile, Linda Fierz-David, a pupil of Jung, published an English edition of her book on Poliphilo's Dream.[23] It contained an analysis of Priestley's autobiography, *Rain upon*

Godshill (1939). In January, Priestley wrote Jung that he felt she would have done better by using his creative work as a basis for her analysis—and not this autobiography. He also told Jung that he had just read a new edition of H. G. Baynes' *Mythology of the Soul*. He enjoyed it but he wished that somebody would publish case histories in which there was less mythology. He hoped that Jung had had time to look at his book *Delight*, which had a great success in England.[24]

Jung apologized to Priestley for not having written earlier.

> I wanted to read your book first and now I have at last completed its lecture. It is a most delightful book and I enjoyed it very much indeed. There are quite a number of things to which I can subscribe immediately, for instance what you say about tobacco!—Now, since yo.r second letter has come, I cannot wait any longer to answer it.
>
> . . . I'm quite astonished that an English version of Mrs. Fierz's attempt should have got into your hands. When—about two years ago—the question of an English translation of her book on Poliphilo's Dream was discussed I insisted that her analysis of your book should be left out in the English edition. I discussed the matter several times with her as well as with Mr. Barrett of the Bollingen Series.
>
> Poliphilo's Dream in itself is an excellent study of 15th Century psychology. I never felt quite happy about her insistence on the comparison with a modern writer. It doesn't add to the better understanding of old Francesco Colonna.—Well all sorts of things seem to be going on behind the screen about which I'm singularly uninformed. Your reaction is quite remarkable and Mrs. Fierz is going to write to you probably quite soon.

Jung said he wished he could send Priestley a recent work of his own in exchange for Priestley's gift, but no new English translation had yet appeared. His publishers (Routledge & Kegan Paul and the Bollingen Foundation) appeared to be taking all the time in the world to get it done.[25]

Priestley had had marital difficulties, and since 1947 had pursued an affair with Jacquetta Hawkes, an archaeologist and a brilliant writer. The story of their love is told in Brome's *J. B. Priestley* and in Hawkes' *A Quest of Love*.[26] Through Priestley, Hawkes was introduced to Jung's work, of which she became a keen student and admirer. In September, 1953, Priestley informed Jung that he had had a divorce (in June); his former wife remarried and he remarried, too. He told Jung of his present wife's keen interest in Jung's work. Hawkes was anxious to meet Jung even as Priestley was eager to renew their acquaintance. The couple were going to southern Germany in late September, and Priestley asked Jung whether they might see him—if only for an hour or two—about the end of September or beginning of October. Otherwise, said Priestley, he would not be visiting Switzerland. He requested that Jung ask his secretary to let Priestley know.[27] The secretary replied that Jung—presently away on his holiday at Bollingen—had asked her to tell Priestley that he would be back in Küsnacht at the beginning of October and he was looking forward to seeing Priestley again.[28] From Titisee, on the beautiful lake of the same name in the Black Forest in southwestern Germany, Priestley cabled Jung on October 2 to inquire whether they could call on him Sunday or Monday.[29]

In 1954, Priestley published two articles supporting Jung, who was deeply touched by his English friend's kindness and understanding. *The Times Literary Supplement* published Priestley's "Jung and the Writer." Priestley began by humorously remarking that many younger writers today appeared to be in the same predicament as was suggested in the refrain of an American comic song of World War I vintage: "When You're All Dressed Up and Nowhere to Go!" They were all dressed up with talent, but seemed to have nowhere to go. They could not turn—as many writers of the 1930s did—to Karl Marx or Sigmund Freud. They had outgrown the existentialist philosopher Jean-Paul Sartre. Yet they clearly needed to be broadened, toughened, and inspired by some thinker. To date, argued Priestley, too few of them had discovered Jung. Jung himself had made several references to what he called "nothing but" philosophies or attitudes of mind; these belonged to theorists who seemed to cut down our horizons, to give us a viewpoint at the expense of the size and complexity of life—to usher us into a smaller universe. To Priestley, an outlook of this sort was anything but helpful to the literary temperament. Marx and Freud might justly be described as "nothing but" thinkers. Significantly, the writers whom either had deeply influenced had offered us nothing yet that looked like great literature.

Priestley presented Jung as a declared enemy of the "nothing but" jailers of the human spirit. Instead of reducing a work of art, Jung had said that in order to understand art's meaning, we have to allow ourselves to be formed just as it had formed the artist, and then we shall also understand what that artist's primal experience was. In Priestley's depiction of it, the Jungian unconscious was not merely negative, indicating what consciousness had forgotten or repressed—a mere lumber room attached to the conscious mind. It was positive, creative, the huge dark sea out of which consciousness emerged but from which it could not separate itself. Jung saw the illusion that it could so separate as the most dangerous of modern man's illusions. Without the unconscious, human relationships were robbed of depth, art was a pretty toy, and religion was so much empty ceremonial and arid moralizing.

From Jung's idea of libido as psychic energy, his use of the principle of opposites in the psyche, and his theory of the libido's movement with emphasis on progression and regression, said Priestley in his article, come ideas of particular value to the writer. There was also his view of myth that he saw as an attempt to describe the inner world of the psyche, not the outer world—a view poetry has long accepted. A young critic of poetry who wished to broaden the base and increase the depth of his or her criticism might do well to study Jung's psychology. So, too, might the religious and social historian. Jung had shown how, when the libido's progressive movement is obstructed, energy in the regressive phase might move—so to speak—in a downward direction, into the depths of the collective unconscious. There it activated primordial and archetypal contents, so gods moved on the mountains, heroes sprang out of caves, and monsters roared in the forests. Whole masses of human beings might find themselves lost in the same mad dream—and not only in ancient history. Jung pointed out that modern man, with belief in the supreme power of consciousness and a secular, non-symbolic style of life, is peculiarly suited to be the victim of this process. So, a contemporary nation that prided itself on its scientific education prostrated itself before a Hitler and committed appalling atrocities. Jung, in the 1920s, himself announced an imminent explosion of the German spirit; his prophecy, Priestley continued, was based on what he had observed in the inner life of his German patients. Our great loss was that his own research did not take him toward an examination and critical analysis of history. We need to reject the stale phrases and trite explanations of our political differences. More and more people were at the mercy of mass communications: an acceptance of the hasty rationalizations of the conscious mind might be more and more dangerous.[30]

The novelist or dramatist concerned with personal relationships could learn from Jung much of value as well. Priestley explained, for example, that Jung called the archetype, or eternal image of woman the "anima," and that of man the "animus." It was an unconscious, hereditary factor of primordial origin. Because it existed in man's unconscious, the anima carried with it a strange compelling magic. Popular fiction and films showed us these anima figures. The timeless and masklike beauty of Greta Garbo made her a wonderfully acceptable anima figure, and of this her producers and directors were obscurely aware. A man who was unaware of his anima would project it onto a living woman—who would then have for him all its compelling magic. This might result in anything from a "mad infatuation" to a long, happy marriage. Turning next to religion, Priestley remarked that we must remember that Jung had not set out in quest of religious experience, but he arrived at it by exploring the depths of the psyche in his innumerable patients, by way of his therapeutic practice, by way of science. His temperament might color his explanations. Yet all our explanations—including those of his critics—are thus colored. Jung had come closer to bridging the great gap of our times than any other thinker. For Priestley, if a writer aspired to anything more than the lightest entertainment, he or she needed to consider the minds and souls of fellow human beings. If he or she felt, as so many writers did, imprisoned by the thought of the times, compelled to be narrower in outlook than he or she wanted to be, chafing against "nothing but" theories, then in Jung the person might find a great liberator.[31]

In *The New Statesman and Nation*, in October, Priestley next reviewed *The Collected Works of C. G. Jung* that had appeared. He considered Jung to be a rare great thinker who did not regard himself as the plaything of a malevolent fate. Priestley described Jung as a "massive, formidable man, but easily roused to laughter," on good terms with this life, in every sense of the term, a big man: a man who was broadly based and proceeded from an excess of energy and sensibility, a "life-enhancer," whose thought and literature came from a fulness of life—one of the greatest in our age. Whatever his popularity in psychological clinics since World War II, Jung had attracted more and more attention outside them—especially among social and religious philosophers. Priestley may have mentioned the latter particularly in view of Jung's *Answer to Job*—at the time about to appear in England. Priestley admitted some bias, but he found that a high proportion of recent books showing insight into contemporary problems and dilemmas contained references to Jung and showed some understanding of his work. In this review, Priestley defended Jung against the most common charge against him: that he was "mystical" or "metaphysical." Priestley sought to explain the charge. Jung's hypothesis of the collective unconscious was indeed bold and startling. But it fitted facts—e.g., the common inheritance of symbols, the fantasies of psychosis—not accounted for by more cautious thinkers. Some of the people who heatedly declared that all talk of collective unconscious was sheer "bosh" were obviously the victims of forces in themselves they could not understand. Nevertheless, doubts and difficulties existed regarding Jung's theory of the collective unconscious. Some of them explain that frequent charge of being "mystical." There were times when Jung wrote as if the unconscious were all-knowing, all-wise, all-purposive. Again, at other times, readers were left somewhat confused about adventures among the archetypes. Still, as readers following every twist and turn of Jung's thought about the collective unconscious, Priestley suggested that we are constantly rewarded. We are given insights of the utmost value into what has moved both individuals and huge masses of human beings, into the arts and into sexual love, into history and into religion. Priestley thought many might find help between the tall covers of these *Collected Works*—covers colored a green-turquoise, like a deep sea in clear sunlight.[32]

Priestley was deeply touched by Jung's expression of gratitude for his two articles: Jung had given his wife and him so much and held such a high place in their thoughts.[33]

Jung was very grateful indeed for Priestley's support, support that had come when it was badly needed. A lack of acceptance of his work in the scientific world and, recently, responses to the German edition of his *Answer to Job* bothered Jung.

> You as a writer are in a position to appreciate what it means to an isolated individual like myself to hear one friendly human voice among the stupid and malevolent noises rising from the scribbler infested jungle. I am indeed most grateful for your warm-hearted support and your generous appreciation. Your succour comes at a time when it is badly needed: soon a little book of mine will be published in

England which my publishers in USA did not dare to print. It's title is: *"Answer to Job"*. It deals with the wholly unsatisfactory outcome of the book of Job and what its further historical consequences for the development of certain religious questions including Christian views were. The book will be highly unwelcome in certain spheres and will be misunderstood and misinterpreted accordingly. The German edition over here has already upset the representatives of three religions, not because it is irreligious, but because it takes their statements and premises seriously. Needless to say that the best of the so-called free-thinkers are equally shocked. Sir Herbert Read who is informed about its contents, wisely said: "You certainly understand how to put the foot into it." But I am really glad that they are willing to print it.[34]

To Upton Sinclair, Jung had expressed himself about his *Answer to Job* as well. In early 1953, he had sent the German edition, *Antwort auf Hiob* (1952), to the American writer. He told Sinclair that the book was rather revolutionary and apt to be misunderstood; indeed, it was already misunderstood to a grotesque degree. A number of theologians, however, thought highly of it.[35] Sinclair had tried to read it, but he had found Jung's German too much for him. When the English edition appeared he read it and was in awe: Jung's wisdom seemed as vast as his knowledge, and his mischievous humor delighted Sinclair. For his part, Sinclair told Jung about his own manuscript, "Enemy in the Mouth," concerning the alcoholic writers he had known, indeed, forty well known writers—the ablest and best. He had been trying for a year, but publishers had not touched it.[36] Jung responded that his *Answer to Job* was left by Bollingen Foundation to the English publishers—they apparently feared something like "Unamerican activities" and the loss of prestige. He felt that his little book would get on its way slowly as all his other work had done. The way in which the "scientific world" reacted reminded him strongly of those times in the first decade of the twentieth century when he had stood up for Freud against a world blindfolded by prejudice. Today—Jung minced no words in saying—some incompetent and profoundly ignorant reviewers sneezed at him. On average, he felt, he got bad reviews, which ought to convince him that he was writing pretty good stuff. Fortunately the public did not heed this inadequate criticism—his books sold satisfactorily. He was sorry to take up Sinclair's valuable time with such personal outpourings, but he wanted to explain why he took bad criticism as something to be expected.[37]

While Jung's *Answer to Job* was in the works, Priestley had been to America to collect material for a joint book with his wife. Jacquetta Hawkes had gone to New Mexico to write imaginatively about the life of primitive people and the surviving native Americans there, while Priestley had visited the new cities of Texas to see what contemporary people were making of their lives. They were entitling the book "Journey Down a Rainbow," for the ladder that led down to the sacred chamber of the kiva of the Pueblos in New Mexico was called a rainbow. If they felt the book was good enough they would dedicate it to Jung.[38] After it was published they sent him a copy.[39] When he received it, he was just leaving for his retreat at Bollingen. He asked his secretary to thank them very much for the book and for the kind dedication. He would write them as soon as he read the work.[40]

On November 27, 1955, Emma Jung died after she became seriously ill in early November. *Journey Down a Rainbow* was the last book that she read—and with great pleasure—before she could read no more. Jung had given her the book since he had very much enjoyed it. For several months after her death, Jung did not look to his correspondence and afterwards it was simply too much for him at the age of 80. This was the reason—his secretary subsequently explained to Priestley—why Priestley had never received an answer from Jung to *Journey Down a Rainbow*.[41]

Jung's correspondence with Priestley ended in 1955. Their friendship endured. When Jung's *Undiscovered Self* was published in 1958 he sent the Priestleys an inscribed copy. They were both very touched to receive it.[42]

Notes

Part I

1. Paul Mellon, *Reflections in a Silver Spoon: A Memoir*, with John Baskett (New York: William Morrow, 1992), 143–45.
2. Ibid., 145–46.
3. Ibid., 157–59. His account of his parents' marriage, separation, and divorce is given in Chapters 2–4.
4. Mary Mellon to Jung, February 24, 1936, Jung Archives, Swiss Federal Institute of Technology, Zurich. Hereafter abbreviated JA.
5. Paul Mellon to Jung, December 6, 1937, JA.
6. Mellon to Jung's secretary, January 10, 1938, JA.
7. Mellon to Marie-Jeanne Schmid, Jung's secretary, March 20, 1938, JA.
8. Mellon, *Reflections in a Silver Spoon*, 162, 164.
9. Ibid., 164–65, 167.
10. Jung to Mary Mellon, September 5, 1939, JA.
11. Mary Mellon to Jung, December 28, 1939, JA.
12. Mellon, *Reflections in a Silver Spoon*, 168.
13. Jung to Mary Mellon, April 7, 1940, JA.
14. William McGuire, *Bollingen: An Adventure in Collecting the Past*, Bollingen Series (Princeton: Princeton University Press, 1982), 3, 33.
15. Jung to Mary Mellon, June 19, 1940, JA. The letter is one of the four letters from Jung to Mary Mellon published in

C. G. Jung: Letters, ed. Gerhard Adler with Aniela Jaffé, vol. 1, Bollingen Series XCV (Princeton: Princeton University Press, 1973). None of Mary's letters to Jung, of course, are in the work.

16. Jung to Mary Mellon, August 21, 1940, JA.

17. Jung to Mary Mellon, October 12, 1940, JA.

18. Jung to Mary Mellon, January 7, 1941, JA. The letter is printed in *C. G. Jung: Letters*, ed. Adler, vol. 1.

19. Mary Mellon to Marie-Jeanne Schmid, February 14, 1941, JA.

20. Schmid to Mary Mellon, March 25, 1941, JA.

21. Jung to Mary Mellon, April 18, 1941, JA. The letter appeared in *C. G. Jung: Letters*, ed. Adler, vol. 1.

22. Telegram from Mary Mellon to Jung [stamped Küsnacht (Zürich), July 26, 1941], JA.

23. Mary Mellon to Jung, August 26, 1941, JA.

24. Dream dated August 14, 1941, enclosure accompanying the letter of Mary Mellon to Jung, August 26, 1941, JA.

25. Mary Mellon to Jung, August 26, 1941, JA.

26. Jung to Mary Mellon, September 8, 1941, JA. The letter appeared in *C. G. Jung: Letters*, ed. Adler, vol. 1. It does not contain, however, the details of Mary's letter of August 26 nor of the dream.

27. Draft of a telegram from Jung to Mary Mellon, dated October 8, 1941, JA.

28. Telegram from Mary Mellon to Jung [stamped Küsnacht (Zürich), November 10, 1941], JA.

29. Cable from Jung to Mary Mellon, n.d., JA.

30. Jung to Mary Mellon, November 18, 1941, JA.

31. Mary Mellon to Jung, November 26, 1941, JA.

32. Jung to Mary Mellon, January 31, 1942, JA.

33. Mary Mellon to Jung, February 20, 1942, JA.

34. Ibid.

35. Ibid., with enclosure, "Tentative List of Publications," JA.

36. Jung to Mary Mellon, April 10, 1942, JA.

37. Ibid.

38. McGuire, *Bollingen*, 52.
39. Mary Mellon to Jung, May 25, 1942, JA.
40. D. D. Shepard to Jung, July 3, 1942, Paul Mellon's Office, Washington, D.C.
41. Telegram from Mary and Paul Mellon to Jung, July 28, 1942, JA.
42. Jung to "Dear Sir," August 14, 1942, JA.
43. McGuire, *Bollingen*, 57.
44. See ibid., 59–60.
45. Telegram from Mary Mellon to Jung, March 22, 1943, JA.
46. Mary Mellon to Jung, n.d. [1943], JA.
47. Ibid.
48. Ibid.
49. Cf. McGuire, *Bollingen*, 72.
50. Telegram from Mary Mellon to Jung, July 29, 1943, JA.
51. Typescript [probably of a telegram], Jung to Mary Mellon, January 3, 1944, JA.
52. Telegram from Mary Mellon to Jung, June 23, 1944, JA.
53. Handwritten copy of a cable from Jung to Mary Mellon. The copy is dated June 27, 1944. The cable was telephoned from Reid's (in Upperville, Virginia) on June 28. JA.
54. Telegram from Mary Mellon to Jung, July 1, 1944, JA.
55. Telegram from Mary Mellon to Jung, July 26, 1944, JA.
56. One page of a typescript of a letter from Eleanor Bertine to Jung, December 10, 1944, among the Jung-Mellon papers, JA. The original letter is also in the Archives. See Aryeh Maidenbaum and Stephen A. Martin, eds., *Lingering Shadows: Jungians, Freudians, and Anti-Semitism* (Boston & London: Shambhala, 1991), on whether Jung was anti-Semitic, and see also pp. 38–39 below. See my *Major Issues in the Life and Work of C. G. Jung* (Lanham, New York, London: University Press of America, 1996) on the issue: was Jung anti-Nazi or, at any time, "a Nazi sympathizer"?
57. A. Haettenschwiller to Mary Mellon, March 29, 1945, JA.
58. Telegram from Mary Mellon to Jung, April 5, 1945, JA.

59. Typescript of a cable from Jung to Mary Mellon, April 10, 1945, JA.

60. Mary's letter is not in the Jung Archives in Zurich nor in Paul Mellon's Office.

61. Jung to Mary Mellon, September 24, 1945, JA. The letter was published in Andrew Samuels' article, "New Material Concerning Jung, Anti-Semitism, and the Nazis," *The Journal of Analytical Psychology*, 38 (October 1993), 463–70, and part of it in his book, *The Political Psyche* (London and New York: Routledge, 1993).

62. Later in his *Memories, Dreams, Reflections* (1962) he gave a much shorter distance—about 1500 km (approximately a thousand miles).

63. Jung to Mary Mellon, September 24, 1945, JA.

64. Jung, "The Psychology of the Transference," in *The Practice of Psychotherapy, Collected Works* 16, pars. 364–65, 367. *Die Psychologie der Übertragung* was published in 1946.

65. Telegram from Mary Mellon to Jung, October 26, 1945, JA.

66. Telegram from Mary Mellon to Jung, October 30, 1945, JA.

67. Typescript of a cable from Jung to Mary Mellon, October 30, 1945, JA.

68. Mary Mellon to Jung, November 10, 1945, JA. Mary's handwritten letters usually leave a space between each line. They are pleasant in appearance and easy to read.

69. Mary Mellon to Jung, November 10, 1945, JA.

70. Ibid.

71. Ibid.

72. Jung to Mary Mellon, December 20, 1945, JA.

73. Mary Mellon to Jung, December 30, 1945, JA.

74. Telegram from Mary Mellon to Jung, January 7, 1946, JA.

75. [Secretary] to Mary Mellon, January 15, 1946, JA.

76. Telegram from Jung to Mary Mellon, January 16 [1946], and a handwritten copy of the same, JA.

77. Telegram from Mary Mellon to Jung, April 6, 1946, JA.

78. Jung to Mary Mellon, April 13, 1946, JA.

79. Mary Mellon to Jung, May 6, 1946, JA.

80. Mary Mellon to Jung, May 10, 1946, JA. This business-like letter is signed: Cordially yours, Mary Mellon. On the letterhead of the Bollingen Series stationery the names of the following appear: Mrs. Paul Mellon, Editor; John D. Barrett, Associate Editor; Huntington Cairns, Consulting Editor; and Pantheon Books, Publishers.

81. Jung to Mary Mellon, May 21, 1946, JA.

82. Mary Mellon to Jung, May 29, 1946, JA. The letter is typed on Bollingen Series stationery.

83. Jung to Mary Mellon, June 3, 1946, JA.

84. John D. Barrett, Associate Editor, to Herbert Read, c/o George Routledge & Sons, June 20, 1946, JA. This formal letter is typed on Bollingen Series stationery.

85. Mary Mellon to Jung, June 24, 1946, JA.

86. McGuire, *Bollingen*, 111, 113.

87. Telegram from Mary Mellon to Jung, July 17, 1946, JA.

88. Mary Mellon to Jung, July 17, 1946, JA. She signed this letter on Bollingen stationery: "With kind regards to you and Mrs. Jung. Cordially yours, Mary Mellon."

89. Jung to Mary Mellon, July 25, 1946, JA. Like her letter of July 17 it is signed "Yours cordially."

90. McGuire, *Bollingen*, 112.

91. Mellon, *Reflections in a Silver Spoon*, 221; McGuire, *Bollingen*, 114.

92. McGuire, *Bollingen*, 114.

93. Telegram from John D. Barrett to Dr. and Mrs. C. G. Jung, received October 13, 1946, JA.

94. Mellon, *Reflections in a Silver Spoon*, 222.

95. Telegram from Paul Mellon to Jung, November 14, 1946, JA.

96. McGuire, *Bollingen*, 123–24, 128–29. Volume 19 was the General Bibliography, and Volume 20 was the General Index.

97. Interview with Franz Jung, July 2, 1993.

Part II

1. Priestley to Jung, May 3, 1946, JA.
2. Jung to Priestley, May 7, 1946, J. B. Priestley Collection, Harry Ransom Humanities Research Center, University of Texas at Austin.
3. Priestley to Jung, May 20, 1946, JA.
4. Jung to Priestley, May 23, 1946, JA.
5. Jung to Priestley, July 17, 1946, JA.
6. Priestley to Jung, July 23, 1946, JA.
7. Jung to Priestley, August 9, 1946, JA.
8. Priestley to Jung, September 4, 1946, JA.
9. Jung's Secretary [Marie-Jeanne Schmid] to Priestley, September 18, 1946, JA.
10. Barbara Hannah, *Jung: His Life and Work: A Biographical Memoir* (New York: G. P. Putnam's Sons, 1976), 186, 293; Gerhard Wehr, *Jung: A Biography*, tr. David M. Weeks (Boston & London: Shambhala, 1987), 357; Frank McLynn, *Carl Gustav Jung* (New York: St. Martin's Press, 1997), 464.
11. Vol. 36, no. 930 (1946): 615–16, 641. In Jung's *Collected Works* 10 (1964), pars. 444–57, it appears slightly revised.
12. "The Fight with the Shadow," *The Listener* (London), November 7, 1946, 615–16.
13. Ibid., 616.
14. Ibid., 616, 641.
15. Mrs. Jane Priestley to Jung, November 14, 1947, JA.
16. Jung to Mrs. Jane Priestley, November 25, 1947, JA.
17. *J. B. Priestley* (London: Hamish Hamilton, 1988), 308–9, 313–16.
18. See Hannah, *Jung*, 297–98, 300.
19. See Brome, *J. B. Priestley*, 300, and n. 23.
20. Jung to Priestley, January 28, 1948, Harry Ransom Humanities Research Center.
21. Jung to Priestley, February 7, 1948, Harry Ransom Humanities Research Center.
22. Jung's Secretary to Priestley, September 24, 1949, JA.

23. Fierz-David, *The Dream of Poliphilo*, tr. Mary Hottinger (New York: Pantheon Books for Bollingen Foundation).

24. Priestley to Jung, January 20, 1950, JA.

25. Jung to Priestley, January 27, 1950, JA.

26. See *J. B. Priestley*, Chapters 22–25; *A Quest of Love* (New York: George Braziller, 1981), 214–20.

27. Priestley to Jung, September 3, 1953, JA.

28. Jung's Secretary to Priestley, September 14, 1953, JA.

29. Telegram from Priestley to Jung, October 2, 1953, JA.

30. Priestley, "Jung and the Writer," *The Times Literary Supplement*, August 6, 1954, iii.

31. Ibid.

32. Priestley, "Books in General," *The New Statesman and Nation*, 48 (October 30, 1954): 541–42. A review of *The Collected Works of C. G. Jung*, vols. 7, 12, 16, 17, tr. R. F. C. Hull (London: Routledge).

33. Priestley to Jung, December 20, 1954, JA.

34. Jung to Priestley, November 8, 1954, JA.

35. Jung to Sinclair, January 12, 1953, JA.

36. Sinclair to Jung, February 5, 1955, JA. See also Sinclair to Jung, December 28, 1954, about Sinclair's manuscript. It was later published under the title *The Cup of Fury* (Great Neck, NY: Channel Press, 1956).

37. Jung to Sinclair, February 25, 1955, JA.

38. Priestley to Jung, December 20, 1954, JA.

39. Priestley to Jung, October 24, 1955, JA.

40. A. Jaffé, Jung's Secretary, to Priestley and Hawkes, November 1, 1955, JA.

41. Aniela Jaffé to Priestley, December 9, 1956, JA.

42. Jacquetta Priestley to Jung, June 19, 1958, JA.

Index